I Never Danced With an Eggplant (On a Streetcar Before)

By Errol Laborde

Foreword by Mel Leavitt

Illustrated by Arthur Nead

PELICAN PUBLISHING COMPANY

Gretna 2000

Table Of Contents

First published, 1988
First Pelican edition, 2000

Foreword

By Mel Leavitt

The people of this magical, mythical island city have an uncanny ability to celebrate themselves. Self-entertaining, they have a genius for making major events out of small occasions, banqueting on life, finding treasures in the most trivial. That's why Errol Laborde qualifies as Big Easy's perfect people's laureate. Snoballs, streetcars, Lucky Dogs, or makin' groceries, he has absorbed this unique and often befuddling city from his City Park childhood. Nobody knows the real New Orleans better. Not even those who, perchance, have danced with an eggplant.

Introduction

It was an opportunity I had been waiting for. Ever since what had been the *Vieux Carre Courier* merged into *Gris-Gris* newspaper, a weekly published out of Baton Rouge, the new *Gris-Gris* had been committed to having a New Orleans feel to it. What better way could there have been than to have Don Lee Keith, a veteran of the *Times-Picayune* and the *Courier* and one of New Orleans' most talented columnists — a writer, incidentally, who I admired very much — write a weekly local color column about life in the state's largest city. As a freelance writer for *Gris-Gris* I may have been Streetcar's biggest fan, always enjoying it while at the same time wishing that I could have the opportunity, not to take Keith's place — for nobody could — but to have such a column of my own.

Then came the phone call, from *Gris-Gris* editor Sandy Branch. Keith was leaving the paper, would I like to take over Streetcar? During high school I paid close attention, on those days when I had to rely on transit to get home from school, to how the streetcar drivers operated their craft — throttle and brake, throttle and brake. Now, in a metaphorical sense (and no other sense would be more appropriate for a newspaper column) I would be at the throttle and not really caring much about the brake.

Streetcar in that context may have lived on indefinitely except that *Gris-Gris* didn't. As happened to many of the so-called "alternative" newspapers that were birthed in the Seventies, *Gris-Gris* (which has since been reincarnated) came to a sudden end. The column became the journalistic equivalent of the defunct Canal streetcar line — derailed and dismantled.

During a two-year stint that followed at *New Orleans Magazine*, a column written by me called "Parade" was quite similar in style and substance to what Streetcar had been. But the limitations of a monthly never allowed this Parade to have the spontaneity that either a column or a real parade for that matter, should have.

Then came another opportunity. In January, 1982 I accepted a position as associate editor of *Gambit*® newspaper — New Orleans' surviving alternative newspaper. In taking the job I wasn't in a position to be too demanding, but I did have one request to make of *Gambit's* editor and founder Gary Esolen. "There's this weekly column I would like to write, it's called Streetcar..."

At this writing Streetcar has continued, never missing a week, except for an occasional vacation break. In the process I am proud to say that it has twice won First Place awards in the New Orleans Press Club's Column category. In 1985 the column earned the Alex Waller Award,

the Press Club's highest honor for writing achievemer.t. Most important, from the reaction I get the column seems to have won a bit of a
following and perhaps a fan or two.

In retrospect the column may have done even bette-, or perhaps far
worse, had it not been for the limitations of four rules that it has followed
more or less faithtfully: One, Streetcar is about life in New Orleans.
Tempting as it might be, it has never strayed out of the region, except
when making a local connection. Two, it is honest; never once reflecting
advertising considerations. When it has boasted of places, such as Hansen's snowball stand or Dixie Beer it has been out of a heartfelt support
for local businesses trying to make it in the city. Three, it has tried to be
consistent to a style — reflective rather than interviewish, and when the
subject allows for it, with attempt at humor. And Four, it has avoided
what I call "beignet journalism" — a reliance on the age-old cliches about
the city. There have been no columns about such overused topics as
Mark Twain's legacy to the river, the call of the vegetable vendor, or the
happy sounds of the riverboat calliope. (There was once, I will confess,
actually a column about the beignet — the fried pastry served with coffee
and chicory at Cafe du Monde in the French Quarter — but that was only
after the state legislature had declared it to be the state doughnut. All of
the above rules, I would assume, might be subject to temporary suspen-
sion, in response to similar acts of wisdom.)

What has, more so than a set of guidelines, had mcre of a favorable
influence on the column has been the support of some very special
people. Primary among them has been my wife Peggy Scott Laborde, to
whom this book is dedicated. She has provided inspiration and
cheerleading for the column and also mastered the right amount of
pressure to get to get this book project moving.

None of what has been written would have been possible, of course,
without my parents Rena and Ellis Laborde, who had the wisdom to raise
me in New Orleans.

That the column has survived is due to Gary Esolen, the four.der and
former editor of *Gambit* who both allowed and tolerated the column
through the years. *Gambit* itself would not have survived were it not for
Phillip Carter, a generous businessman from a rightfully proud journalistic family who carried much of the financial burden of the paper
during those hard formative years. That the paper still survives is due to
the wisdom and intercession of Landmark Publishing Company and its
vice-president for special publications, George Brooks.

All of the above get credit in part for having provided the setting for
the astonishingly talented collection of people who comprise *Gambit*.
Like the trolley, this Streetcar would have never gotten very far without
the support staff. Thanks to those people who through the years have
typed, proofed (while tolerating my typing), offered suggestions and

pasted up the column. There have been many, but none so special as Geraldine Wyckoff, Teresa Askew, Jackie Miller, Sue Barker and Nick Marinello.

One former *Gambit* staff member has given the column its distinctive look. Artist Arthur Nead has, through the years, illustrated the column, as he did the cover of this book, developing a style that has, perhaps more so than the writing (sniff), become the image, and maybe even the appeal, of Streetcar.

If Streetcar deals occasionally in local color, Tom Fitzmorris personifies it all the time. Fitzmorris, who publishes his own magazine *Menu*, is bright, articulate, witty and outspoken, all the better to have made him the city's best known, either by his name or as "Mr. Food," food critic. It was his interest in this project as well as his resources and expertise that have made this book possible.

Every project seems to, at some point, have to involve some legalities, a task handled with speed and good cheer by Nancy Scott Deagan, attorney-at-law and, what is even more important to me, sister-in-law.

There is one more person to be mentioned, most appropriately via an anecdote. Most weeks the ideas for Streetcar topics flow easily, occasionally, however, there is a strain. It happened one day not too long ago that with deadline approaching I still hadn't found an idea that I felt would work. By then I had been writing the column for more than four years and the past seemed to have already stolen all of the doable themes. I decided to use my lunchtime that day to walk the streets of the French Quarter in pursuit of an idea. Surely there would be something that would inspire. So I traversed the old city blocks slowly gazing, looking around, caught in that trance of someone whose search was so futile that the mind begins to wander. But then suddenly that trance was broken by a blast from an automobile horn and the sound of the vehicle pulling up beside me. The man within rolled down his window, laughed then hollered, "Keep looking Errol, you'll find it," he said — and then he drove away. It was Don Lee Keith, and he somehow knew exactly what I was doing. He had no doubt gone through the same many times before. At that moment I felt not only a certain fellowship among people who have written Streetcar, but I also felt a bit wiser: No subject is ever exhausted, especially when the subject — in Streetcar's case, New Orleans — is something that the writer feels so strongly about. A hundred or so columns have been written since that day; a hundred or so more topics realized. And never since then have I had cause to doubt that New Orleans would ever fail to provide another story to be told.

For as long as Streetcar lasts I will gladly take Keith's advice to keep looking and to do so with the confidence that I will indeed find what I am looking for. — *Errol Laborde.*

About The Title

I Never Danced With An Eggplant — On A Streetcar?

In fact, as best as I can recall, I've never danced with an eggplant anywhere at all. The title comes from a line in one of the columns in the Mardi Gras chapter. It tells about a ride on Twelfth Night, January 6, a date that is special in New Orleans as it is the beginning of the Carnival season. On that particular evening a group of revelers, fully costumed, took their traditional streetcar ride to announce to the world — or at least that segment of it waiting at trolley stops — that the Carnival season had arrived. While the streetcar rolled, a band played to which the riders crowded the narrow aisle gyrating to the music. At that point I noticed that the woman I was suddenly dancing with, an otherwise sane friend and neighbor, Callie Cooper, was dressed like an eggplant. "Hmm, I thought, "I never danced. . ." Better yet, read the column.

**To Peggy Scott Laborde,
who never ceases to love.**

CARNIVAL

The Corner

This is a story about a search for a street corner — actually, it's really two street corners, and one didn't require much of a search. In fact, I can see the corner as I write this merely by looking through the window here at Gambit — it's the corner of Rampart and Dumaine. The other corner, St. Claude and Dumaine, is a bit more difficult to find, but what I'm really searching for isn't physical location as much as historic significance.

This search is spurred on by the time of the year and by Professor Longhair's contribution to carnival, his song, "Going to the Mardi Gras." These are the days when the record is being played again. Like azaleas, it blossoms around town once a year. The song has made the corner of St. Claude and Dumaine perhaps the most popular in the city because that's where, "Fess" sang to us, "you will see the Zulu King."

In an earlier, less well-known version, Longhair had the krewe's monarch spotted on Rampart and Dumaine. Just why he shifted the site no one seems to know, nor is there explanation why he picked those corners. That's why I've been searching.

To begin with, just where is the corner of St. Claude and Dumaine? Actually, it's a trick question. The corner doesn't exist anymore. The point where the two streets would intersect is somewhere in what is now Armstrong Park. The city's most heralded intersection is now a patch of green.

That corner, however, would have at one time been amidst a lively mixed neighborhood near the edge of Storyville. Coincidentally, it would have also been near the Green Room, a bar popularized by Al Johnson in the opening of another Mardi Gras rhythm and blues era song, "Carnival Time." "The Green Room is jumping and the place is burning down," Johnson wails, "throw my baby out the window and let the joint burn down, all because it's carnival ti-i-i-me."

None of this explains exactly why the Professor picked the corner to popularize, although he may have been a bit of a prophet. Near where the intersection would be now stands the statue of Louis Armstrong — a past Zulu king. In a sort of figurative sense Longhair was right: Any time all year round you can see a Zulu king, "down on St. Claude and Dumaine."

As for the other corner, Rampart and Dumaine, I have a clue, or at least a hunch, why Longhair selected it. On one sector of the corner stood Cosimo Matassa's J&M Studios, the spot where performers such as Fats Domino, Little Richard, and the Professor stepped before the microphone.

Who knows? Maybe one day before a recording session Longhair looked out this window to my right, noticed the street sign, and thought to himself, "Rampart and Dumaine — mmm."

If someone wants to spot the Zulu king this Mardi Gras, he would have better luck on Rampart and Canal than on any corner mentioned in the songs. Time has created some visual inaccuracies, but the record is still a local classic, enriched by its piano beat introduced by Longhair's now familiar whistling prelude. Perhaps Fess knew that carnival is not just to be appreciated for its sights, but also for its sounds.

The Catch

At 7:18:02, Alvin spotted in the air a bundle of beads and some doubloons that had been thrown from a passing float and seemed to be heading in his direction. In an instant, his hands, which had been tucked in his side pants pockets, shot out like Minuteman missiles newly launched.

As his fists ascended, he instinctively rocked back on both heels, then rolled forward so that the front of his feet could serve as springs to propel his body, poised in a squat position ready for blastoff, above the crowd.

His raised his arms first served as a shield to protect him from the foreign objects speeding in his direction, but then his fists suddenly began to open — sprouting fingers and palms which turned in the direction of the invaders as though guided by radar. The computer within Alvin's mind had instantly changed his upper limbs and digits from shields to interceptors. The mission was clear — to snag the flying objects rather than merely defend himself from them.

His eyes were like beams affixed to prey. The cluster of beads was by then in the downside of an arch and heading towards him. A few pairs had broken from the cluster but most remained intact. Meanwhile, the doubloons had developed separate flight patterns reminiscent of the Blue Angels performing precision drills. One doubloon had dived off to the right. Another had climbed, only to be the victim of an unfortunate collision with a power line, and was tumbling towards the ground; another was heading towards Alvin's left, causing his mental command center to order his left hand to move in that direction, although the timing had been miscalculated. The doubloon slammed into Alvin's elbow then fell towards the concrete.

Quickly, the left arm swung back towards the right limb which by this time was fully extended forward.

Alvin had reached the peak of his leap, and his arms stretched to the maximum as the speeding projectile reached his range. But all around him other bodies were ascending and other arms extending. The air space was not to be his alone.

Below, the falling doubloon performed a last ricochet off his knee, as though to tease him before it hit the ground. But the real action was up above, where Alvin flexed his fingers, grabbing the bead cluster like a pelican snaring a fish.

It was his moment of conquest, but as he began his descent Alvin noticed that he wasn't alone. Two other hands, each connected to a different person, were attached to ends of the cluster. So, as Alvin's feet again touched Mother Earth his left hand swung in to lay further claim to the beads. With the force of both hands, Alvin pushed the beads to his gut and assumed the squatting position, momentarily reliving his grade school basketball days when he grabbed the rebounds. He pointed his elbows outward forming blades to ward off the competing hands, as though he faced the danger that some carnival referee might call, "Jump beads!" There must have been fear in his pose and meanness in his eye because his two opponents suddenly let go of their claim, leaving Alvin with the booty all for his own.

But his victory was not complete. Below, he could hear a tingling sound mixed with the noise of feet shuffling as if they were stomping out an ant hill. The errant doubloon had landed on its edge and was rolling along the concrete, while feet of all sizes tried to stomp it into submission. Alvin pivoted on his right heel and then slapped down the toe-end of his foot just as the doubloon rolled in its way. The coin was trapped beneath his foot as other misguided feet landed nearby. Alvin stepped firmly on the doubloon to assure that no fiend would sneak beneath his sole to snatch it.

He stood there in his moment of victory with beads in hand and doubloon under foot. The time was 7:18:09, less than a second since he had first spotted the throws coming his way.

Suddenly he realized what had happened. He had come to the parade not planning to be an active participant. But then it became infectious. He had reacted first out of the instinct to defend himself and then out of the need to prove himself.

He surveyed his prize and then offered it to a nearby child after concluding that he had no use for it.

For him the satisfaction had come not from the trophy but from the thrill of the catch.

Twelfth Night

Skippy the Clown was crying — or, at least, he seemed to be, as the streetcar he was in rolled along St. Charles Avenue. He seemed sad because the band at the back of the streetcar, the Storyville Stompers, was playing a funeral dirge. While the band played, Skippy led a procession down the center aisle of the streetcar. Following him were his colleagues: Kissee the Clown, then a rabbit, a cowgirl, an Arab or two, an Ignatius Reilly look-alike and miscellaneous sequined undefinables.

As he shuffled down the aisle, Skippy waved a paper napkin in the air, representative of the rag needed to dry his tears. Those behind him each reached for the napkin pack next to the tray of muffulettas and followed the actions of their leader. Skippy let out a groan; so did others, in what was one of the more bizarre funeral processions to be staged in a city already known for making sport out of dismissing the deceased. But as Skippy and friends wailed, those who had heard the dirge before could expect something was about to happen — and it did. With a roll of the drum, the Stompers changed their tempo and the dirge became second-lining music to which Skippy began waving his napkin joyously while jumping down the aisle, pausing only to say of the deceased, "I never liked him that much anyway."

Actually, there wasn't much to like, because the deceased never existed except maybe in a symbolic sense, since it was January 6, the evening of Twelfth Night, and Skippy and friends were witnessing the demise of the Christmas season and celebrating the rebirth of carnival time in New Orleans.

Skippy belongs to the Phunny Phorty Phellows, a recent restoration of a 19th century carnival group that always marched to a different drum. In their new life, the Phellows have taken to themselves the responsibility of packing into a streetcar on the evening of Twelfth Night to announce to the city the arrival of carnival. Thus it happened that unsuspecting tourists waiting for a streetcar watched in awe as a trolley carrying a pirate dancing with Pancho Villa rolled past them.

"I've never danced with an eggplant in a streetcar before," one Phellow (they're really not all fellows) told his dance partner of the moment, who was dressed in a baggy purple costume topped with a fox fur collar to represent an eggplant with frostbite. "You haven't?" she replied. "And I thought everybody had."

Such are the discoveries one makes on a day that means more in New Orleans than in most other places in the world — January 6, the last day of Christmas, the beginning of the carnival season. It is a day of tradition, but quiet tradition practiced by a few. Thus, on that evening, one local gourmet makes his customary trek to Arnaud's, where he orders the Rock Cornish game hen flambe a la Twelfth Night.

An artist in the French Quarter sent out Twelfth Night cards rejoicing that while the rest of the world slips towards "Orwellian techno-depersonalization," we in New Orleans "remain carelessly safe from homogeneity. We have magic."

At the Municipal Auditorium, the Twelfth Night Revelers recreate their century-old ritual as their monarch, The Lord of Misrule, greets the season.

At the bakeries, the shelves are again stacked with king cakes while the ageless discussion of who makes the best cake begins again.

And the Phellows close their evening over dinner by saluting their monarchs, a Boss and a Queen, who won their station during the streetcar ride by each acquiring one of the dolls packed into the two king cakes.

Yielding to demands from her krewe that she speak, the new Queen told the Phellows that she had just called her out-of-town parents to tell them her good news. "Oh," one parent replied, "your pipes are fixed from the freeze." "No," she answered, "I didn't say, 'I'm clean.' I said, 'I'm queen.'"

Carnival had arrived.

Glowing In The Dark

Even those who lead the parade are sometimes vulnerable to those who merely watch. The WGSO parade progress car was slowing for a moment as the head of the Momus parade reached the corner of St. Charles Avenue and First Street. Riding in the shotgun position, I was the natural choice to make the quick dash for the junk food truck parked on the corner.

Tom Fitzmorris, known to some as Mr. Food, was doing the parade reports that night and had invited me along for the ride. In the early moments of the parade he was going through, as someone might expect of a person nicknamed "Food," a form of popcorn reaction. His habit needed to be fixed.

I ran towards the truck, handed over a dollar, and waited for the popcorn. While waiting, I habitually felt for my wallet. It was gone. Somewhere between the car, which was now starting to move, and the truck, among hundreds of people, my wallet had fallen. I ran back towards the car while staring at the ground. The parade was suddenly quite irrelevant. Nevertheless, it was moving, so I wouldn't have time for a thorough search. I began to run faster towards the car. The night was ruined.

Suddenly a girl, probably in her teens, ran up to me. She recited what has to be the most beautiful of all phrases, "Hey mister, here's your wallet." I grabbed the wallet and took off towards the moving car while muttering what in retrospect must have seemed like an ungrateful "thank you." It wasn't ungrateful, it was just hurried. Suddenly Momus was important again, and the night was beautiful.

From the inside of a Mardi Gras parade looking out, the human mixture that sets a city apart from the suburbs was on display. At first the streets were lined with preppies as the parade rolled beyond

Napoleon Avenue. Then for a few blocks the crowd was mostly black, then mixed, then white again. At one point five girls stood side by side waving, having a good time — each was pregnant. We were passing a few blocks away from a home for unwed mothers.

Occasionally, people waved from the balconies of gracious mansions or from reviewing stands. Others had to be content with the curb as their base.

Near Lee Circle the crowd was much older, having come from nearby retirement homes. Along the first few blocks of the business district the spectators could best be described as "less fortunate." Many were disheveled, with dirty faces but with wide, though toothless smiles. The beautiful people had gathered at Gallier Hall for the annual mayor's reception. Ladies in evening dresses and men in black tie waved properly.

Towards Canal Street the crowd thickened. There were college age couples, then blocks of tourists identifiable by their group badges. One floor above Canal, the socially prominent of the Boston Club gathered on the reviewing stand preparing to meet this year's Momus, a person of secret identity who on another night might be one of them.

As the parade turned from Canal towards Rampart the crowd was again predominately black. It stayed that way until the last few blocks before Armstrong Park, where the clientele from the gay bars came to watch.

It was quite a mixture along the parade route — by race, income, social standing and sexual predilection. But among all those people there was something that united them. It wasn't necessarily truth, justice, spirit or anything corny like that; it was a common craving for one thing — doubloons — not just any doubloons, but specially coined Popeyes Fried Chicken two-for-the-price-of-one doubloons. All along the route people approached us, like peasants in Jakarta, begging pleading for doubloons. We didn't have any. In defense to both taste and tradition, such commercialism is outlawed in parades within the city limits. All we could offer was a wave. Waves, of course, are nice, but they don't buy chicken.

A second common trait of the crowd was the need to prove itself to us. Throughout the evening, spectators yelled of their familiarity with the station. One girl, whose affections obviously belonged to the rock stations, thought enough to holler, "My mama listens to your station." Another shouted, "I watch y'all every night".

Instead of watching the radio, the girl could have found the crowd around her much more fascinating. The city glowed that night. It glowed because thousands of people were out, side-by-side, presumably enjoying themselves. And, to me at least, it glowed not only because Momus had made the evening, but because somewhere out there in the crowd there was a girl who had saved it.

The Final Hours

Here's a case study on how Mardi Gras works.

It was Mardi Gras evening and the mayor was toasting Comus in front of Gallier Hall. Looking on was a masked figure on horseback — the Comus captain. In real life, the captain is a prominent attorney who has been at well-publicized odds with the mayor during the past year. Comus, on the other hand, was this year portrayed by a businessman who, in addition to being a captain of another blue-blooded krewe, headed a special task force for the mayor.

Moments earlier, the mayor had proposed a series of toasts to the police who marched in the parade. Those toasts, made during the last parade of the carnival season, have become the city's symbolic gesture towards thanking the police for their carnival efforts. There is no small irony in the cops sipping Champagne sent from the man who broke their Mardi Gras strike three years ago.

After the parade, and a few blocks along St. Charles Avenue near the corner of Canal Street, a crowd gathered outside the Pickwick Club. The Comus Queen and her court were leaving the club's reviewing stand for the ball. The spectators were mostly ragged; peasants watching the Queen pass by. One young man, with the look and presence of skid row, seemed wide-eyed about it all. He, like the others, waited to discover if seeing a Queen was really such a big deal.

Just as the doors to the Pickwick Club began to open, a streetsweeper charged along St. Charles, scrubbing the stain of the parades. The sweeper sent a wave of water chasing at the ankles of the spectators. Meanwhile, the doorman signaled for the limousine to move close to the curb. The young man from skid row sensed the situation and in all earnestness announced to no one in particular, "We don't want the Queen to get her feet wet."

Soon the Queen appeared and entered the car to the sound of a polite applause. She would soon be off to the ball, where she would join Comus and the captain in bringing an end to carnival.

Meanwhile, the Mayor had completed, for a while, his ceremonial duties. He no doubt had other things on his mind.

And the young man was free to wander along the now empty streets back to where he had come from.

Fantasy had brought together political power and social prominence that evening, as well as like and dislike and wealth and poverty. As the clock rushed to midnight, all the elements were coming back to reality.

A Winter Ritual

A valet wearing a white waistcoat worked continually backstage at the auditorium helping men in and out of their costumes. A button here, a snap there, a tug at the boots, and a businessman was someone else.

Across the room, a bartender heard orders for mixed drinks over the shouts of a krewe lieutenant arranging the maskers for the tableau. "Bloody Mary." "Group one exit from the door to my left." "Give me a refill. " "The tableau starts in five minutes." "Scotch and soda."

A janitor sat quietly near the doorway. Dukes and captains and kings passed his way, but he'd seen it all before. Many times he'd heard that moment when the whistle blows, the house lights dim, the band begins, the spotlight projects — shining on a girl in white escorted by a man in black.

It is the winter ritual of old cities, those aged enough to have an established class of older family names. It is the promenade of high society, debuting the latest crop of young women. As they make the circle along the edge of the auditorium floor proud mamas and aunts applaud. Nearby, maskers hoot good-naturedly. It is strange, this ordeal. The young act as adults, adults like the young. The maskers continue the hooting. You're a lady, heart, but men will be men.

With the debutantes presented, the drum rolls and the spotlights aim at the parting curtain. Suddenly there is a life-size cardboard version of the throne room at the Versailles palace. The crowd applauds at the king standing near his royal chair. From among those masked businessmen one has ascended for the night. He waves his scepter and his subjects cheer.

There's another drum roll and a bit of fanfare. All eyes are now on a debutante who has also ascended. The audience stands as the Queen enters the room. She circles the room while little girls behind her straighten her train at every turn. Her everyday dream of majoring in pre-med and the frustration of trying to understand computers is put aside. Tonight she reigns. Tonight she is the chosen's chosen. The dance lessons, the schooling in charm and etiquette, the uptown education, this is the evening when they must come together to make one perfect lady.

With the rulers seated on their throne, the captain signals that the dancing must begin. On cue, Rene Louapre flips the dance card (this is number one) and signals his band to begin. Women are escorted to meet their masked men, who extended "callout" invitations to them.

From the second level, a first-time observer may wonder what this is all about — people bowing, clapping, and dancing. What it's about is what they don't see. Behind the curtains, society's men have reached the solitude of the backstage. Drinks are poured. Hands are shaken. Connections made. It's business as usual. On the floor, the girls in white have not only entered high society but have been given a head start.

When Louapre flips the card to signal the ninth dance, the floor becomes more crowded. The last few numbers are for general dancing, allowing the waiting gentry to take the floor. Masked men in full dress escort their ladies to dance. "If you can make it there, you can make it anywhere" — Louapre's band plays, "New York, New York." Couples glide across the floor. Others greet the king and queen. "Scotch and soda," someone backstage shouts, while being helped out of his costume.

After the eleventh dance the music stops. The crowd is thin by then, as the rulers and their court head for the limousines waiting to take them to the krewe supper. The monarchs are like Cinderellas, hurrying through the last hours of their reign as though midnight is chasing after them.

Meanwhile, back at the auditorium, the valet finishes packing the costumes. The bartender caps the last scotch bottle and the janitor follows the queen's path, this time with a push mop.

Tomorrow the winter rituals continue. There will be a new queen and a new king. The valet, bartender and janitor will be there too, but unlike those whom they serve, they never have to race with midnight.

Stormy Knights

It was the evening of the grand race, the Knights of Babylon versus the elements. "There will be storms and heavy winds," the voice on the radio warned, "best stay home."

But Knights are not known for their cowardice. "Babylon is on the way," a parade progress reporter announced. "It started 25 minutes early and it's going to try to beat the rain."

St. Charles Avenue was a raceway that night as two traits of New Orleans life, parades and storms, competed. Storms usually win, but the Knights were ready for the fight.

"Babylon is really moving fast," the reporter told, "it's already at Louisiana Avenue."

Never mind that much of the generally jammed parade route was empty, a tribute to the threat of the coming deluge. Almost as though word that the giant was coming had spread through town, the streets were vacant — the timid stayed indoors. But to the Knights, serving in a kingdom where parades are primarily a ritual and only secondarily an entertainment, it didn't matter that the spectators had scattered. The ritual must still be conducted. Besides, someone had to face the invader.

"They will not make the loop on Canal Street," the reporter added. "The parade will head straight down Rampart to the auditorium. This parade is really moving, it should be over by eight o'clock."

Those who peeped through their windows saw a neon blur — a colorful, indeed beautiful parade, telling the story of Kismet, galloping down the street like a pack of peacocks being chased.

"Babylon has just turned onto Rampart," the radio announcer reported. "The parade will be reaching the auditorium soon."

A crowd gathered at the finish line. Rampart is a street of people with no qualms about standing in the rain amidst a potential storm to watch a parade — people who see storms not as a force to drive them inside but as an opportunity to slosh in the rain. For their determination, the people of Rampart would get to witness the race's outcome.

There was no need for radio reports any more. A band marching at double time heralded the arrival, sounding like the cavalry preceding the charge. The musicians' music was accompanied by the sound of their white shoes splashing in the puddles. The race was going to be close.

Next came dukes, riding with heads up as though to show that the enemy had not overcome them. Babylon's King Sargon rolled past his subjects. There might be a storm coming, but it was still his reign.

More bands, then floats. The maskers on board peered down on hundreds of hands sticking out from a wave of umbrellas. Another wave could be seen coming down the street — a group of second-liners danced in the rain, waving the umbrellas in the air while marching alongside a high school band. The lights, the music, the second-lining — the rain. There was no respect for bad weather along North Rampart, its dignity was being defied.

A policeman on a traffic platform only insulted the weather even further. As the bands passed he swayed, jived and applauded, without recognizing that the weather was supposed to be unpleasant.

From his stand he could see the blinking lights approaching. The last float was turning towards the auditorium; the police units and clean-up crews were following close behind. The waterlogged people of Rampart Street walked away with their pockets bulging with beads and doubloons.

Alongside the auditorium, damp maskers climbed off the floats. There was still the ball to attend, but there was also extra time to allow drying. It was only eight o'clock. There would be a full hour to contemplate their adventure and perhaps listen to the howling from outside.

As the floats were being pulled away, the storm was releasing its payload of rain, thunder and winds. But for all the force it could muster, that night nature would only be second best.

Ash Wednesday

On the afternoon of Mardi Gras, a full face mask, once finely outlined with bright feathers, stood smoldering on the concrete of Canal Street. "Is that symbolic of the passing of carnival?" someone asked its owner. "No," the unmasked masker responded, "I just got too close to it with my cigarette.

Had someone been looking for a symbolic passing of carnival they could have waited until that evening, when the weather turned gray.

If weather could be controlled as though run by a computer, no programmer could have improved on the climate of Lent's arrival. The rains held back throughout the day of Mardi Gras, even delaying to let Comus ride. But just as the Mystick Krewe's last float reached the auditorium the condensation became drops. The sky was heavy, the wind was wicked, the time for feasting had ended; the thunderclouds announced that now it was time for penance.

Ash Wednesday in New Orleans should always be a dark, rainy day as the city undergoes a cleansing rite. A priest lifts his finger and gently leaves a cross-shaped smudge on foreheads — a smudge made from ashes. A street cleaner performs his own ritual by scooping carnival's trash from a curb. To dust thou shall return.

Perhaps because New Orleans puts so much celebrating into the coming of Lent, the repentant season itself seems to have more local significance, though the reaction to Lent is hardly one of penance. Ash Wednesday in Catholic New Orleans was a day of seafood, the oyster poor boy picked up on the way from church. It was a time for Sicilian ladies to stuff their artichokes while thinking ahead to their preparations for the St. Joseph's Day altars. It was a day of consulting the church calendar to see if there was a whole or half fish, signifying whether meat should be abstained from for one or two meals. It was a day of resolutions and the inevitable classroom joke of giving up school for Lent.

Lent meant more when the rules were tougher, but what it meant wasn't necessarily tougher rules. Sacrificing pork chops for boiled shrimp was suffering one could easily endure. But religion aside, Lent in New Orleans has always seemed to represent a cleansing — not only of the streets but of the spirit. It tugs at the Puritan ethic — you've had your play, now let's get serious.

As I walked through the Quarter on the day after Mardi Gras that cleansing seemed most evident. The pastel drawings were being washed off the Presbytere, balconies were being hosed, stores were being replenished. Everywhere else life was continuing; here it was fresh again.

It was on an Ash Wednesday that I once heard a street singer wailing soulfully to "Summertime." As she sang, her infant son began to whine. Without missing a note or looking away, the woman reached for the child and slowly carried him to her chest, completing the move just in time to look down at the baby while delivering the song's final line — "hush, little baby, don't you cry." The child in all of us just needs an occasional change of position. Feasting without fasting becomes a burden more than a pleasure.

It rained throughout Ash Wednesday, lasting well beyond midnight and more than 24 hours after Comus' last bow. But on the day after Ash Wednesday the sky was bright blue and the temperature a sweaterless pleasant. The streets were clean and the ashes had presumably been washed from the foreheads. The cleansing was over, but the dust would surely return.

A Ceremonial Palace

Momus himself, whose float had just pulled alongside Gallier Hall, stopped to toast the city and those who represented it that night. After praising the police and the sanitation department, Momus of 1984 added that he hoped he hadn't forgotten anyone but explained that he wasn't used to making speeches through a mask, especially while at the same time his crown was falling off his head. He shouldn't have worried. Over the last 130 years there have been many loose crowns worn at the former City Hall, and not all by carnival monarchs.

Few cities have such a ceremonial palace as does New Orleans, which has made its stately former seat of government a permanent site for pomp under any circumstance. Thus it is that on the evenings of carnival, men in tuxedoes and women in ball gowns walk down the long halls, where pictures hang of former mayors who also participated in the carnival rituals going back even as far as the day in 1872 when a fledgling parade known as Rex greeted, at Gallier Hall, the visiting Russian Archduke Alexis, in whose honor the parade was organized.

There was a time, in the early 1960s, when the parades bypassed Gallier Hall, having been re-routed to stop in front of the then-new City Hall on Perdido Street. But the route change was too far out of the way, besides the rectangular box that was City Hall hardly matched the Greek Temple designed by James Gallier to which the parades were returned, probably forever. It is now chiseled into carnival tradition that representatives of the state and society travel to Gallier Hall, maybe by limousine or by float, and, as though the building is a neutral site, toast each other.

For those groups somewhat affectionately known as the "blue blood" krewes, the stop at Gallier Hall is merely a place to pay respects to the city on the way to greeting queens and courts at nearby private clubs. For other krewes, the Hall serves as a poor man's Boston Club — a place where their consorts and dignitaries can be toasted and duly honored. It is the ultimate in city services, providing a spot in a reviewing stand from which to reign for an evening.

Momus did not need such a service because his Queen waited ahead at the next stop on Canal Street. Hence, his attention was given entirely to praising the city and all those who run it. Momus presented a gift to the mayor's representative and his wife; the official responded by giving Momus a key to the city which would "open any door for you tonight, Your Majesty." Those who still cling to the myths of carnival elitism could take note that politically prominent blacks and high society whites were getting along famously that evening. That may be a legacy of Gallier Hall, a historically political building, where power and prestige have intermingled for so long. Those who have had either know that opportunities to share the Champagne and honor others should not be ignored, because no crown is totally secure.

A Butterfly Of Winter

Sometime this carnival, someone somewhere should lift a toast to the memory of Perry Young — especially those who appreciate the history, tradition and grace of the New Orleans carnival, those who celebrate the season in grand uptown parlors or backstage at the ball, or those who simply keep hours at library tables, studying the season's past. They should drink to Perry Young because through him we know much more about carnival's history; although little about the man himself.

Perry Swearingen Young was a journalist in New Orleans during the 1920s and '30s. He was a good writer who produced a local classic, *The Mystic Krewe: Chronicles of Comus and His Kin* — probably the most important book ever written about the origins of the early carnival. All research about the season properly begins with a reading of the book. But Young was one of those writers saddened by never knowing his success. Although 45 years after his death *The Mystick Krewe* remains timeless, he died without reaping any profit from the book, nor likely realizing its importance.

Young was born in Abilene, Texas, not a likely beginning for someone who would receive a bachelor of arts degree from Yale and become a chronicler of New Orleans society. He graduated from Yale in 1909, then headed back to Texas, where he held maritime reporting jobs with the Galveston Tribune and the Houston Post before being drawn into World War I, an adventure which was followed by his inaugurating Gulf Ports magazine, a publication headquartered in New Orleans. Having established himself in this city, Young, in 1924, shifted to editing another port-related house organ, World Port, the monthly publication of the American Association of Port Authorities. Between then and 1933 he also opened his own business, Carnival Press, the name under which he wrote, edited and published carnival programs. Both World Port and Carnival Press were operated out of the same office at 520 Whitney Bank Building, a spot which became the informal cradle of carnival history.

There are many gaps to Young's story, but it might be supposed that in writing about ports, and in being named public relations agent for the Dock Board, his circle included many of the city's prominent citizens, some of whom were part of the social side of carnival. Young had contacts in the Comus organization to the extent that he wrote the krewe's programs. The author himself belonged to Alexis, at the time a very prominent social organization. He was also invited to join the Pickwick Club, and might have belonged to Comus. But his best offer came when he arranged with the Captain of Comus, Sylvester P. Walmsley, to do a history of the Mystick Krewe — the group that founded and maintained the New Orleans parading tradition. The book was to be prepared as a krewe gift to celebrate the group's 75th anniversary in 1932. It was a prize that even seemed worthy of press coverage such as by New Orleans *States* columnist (later congressman) F. Edward Hebert, who reported on Jan. 6 of that year that those in Comus' favor would receive the book.

But then Young's career took a different turn. Walmsley had died and the interim Comus captain had decided against the book. These were also hard times in the real world, as the glitter of carnival was paled by the depression. World Port magazine was moved to California, leaving its editor behind. Young maintained Carnival Press and also began publishing two other magazines, Shore and Beach and Garden. But the income was not steady.

His daughter, Zuma Young Salaun, recalls that there was financial uneasiness during that time, but that her father was too proud to discuss his problems at home. "My mother wanted him to find a job like a streetcar driver," she remembered, "but he wasn't very mechanical, he would have wrecked the streetcar."

Instead, the writer in him tried to prevail, churning out house organs and writing carnival publications, some of which could contend with The Mystick Krewe for thoroughness and style. He was trained in the classics, mythology and foreign languages, making him the right reporter to break through the lore from which carnival grew. He wrote with a scholar's familiarity of the poet Ovid's description of the early pagan rites of spring. He collected engravings of early parades and listed those long-forgotten who wore the crowns. His was a journal of New Orleans society written and presented in a style to embellish the grandest of reading room coffeetables.

Young died in 1939 at the age of 51. Only about 1000 copies of his book had been distributed. In a warehouse, his daughter located approximately 9,000 unbound copies, from which she was able to distribute some of the engravings. Eventually, the remaining stock was sold for waste paper.

In 1969, Zuma Young Salaun allowed the book to be reprinted. Having survived legal skirmishes with a publisher, Salaun claims to have regained control of the reprint, some copies of which are still stacked in her closet. She had become a carnival historian on her own, giving lectures, writing pamphlets, and remembering her father.

After his death, Perry Young was eulogized not so much as an historian as a conservationist. Of his writings in Shore and Beach, for example, it was said that, "the cause of shore protection lost a valiant and gallant advocate... who did not strive for wealth."

But Perry Young's memory has been preserved by Mardi Gras, and he will forever be remembered each winter for his book — a study which contains in its very opening what to me may be the most beautiful description of carnival ever written:

"Carnival is a butterfly of winter, whose last mad flight of Mardi Gras forever ends his glory. Another season is the glory of another butterfly, and the tattered, scattered, fragments of rainbow wings are in turn the record of his day."

Many seasons have passed since Perry Young completed The Mystick Krewe. Now there is a new generation of writers covering carnival, any one of whom would be fortunate to one day look at the spectacle and see a butterfly.

Charlie's Evening

It was 8:40 in the evening when the last unit of the parade passed the store where Charlie worked. Charlie was a night watchman, and his evenings were usually spent in silence. The front display window was his porthole to the world, but it was a world populated only by passing cars and trucks; its only music was of engines and sirens.

On this night, however, there had been real music and people and color to break the monotony. But as the parade marched away, Charlie noticed that his world looked different now. It was speckled with paper plates, cups, chicken bones, cellophane bags, and the unmistakable orange stripes of Popeyes wrappers. There wasn't much to Charlie's world, but at 8:41 that evening, what there was of it looked like a war zone, and his side had lost.

At 8:42, there was noise outside as though a battle had begun. Charlie stared out his window and noticed a platoon of tank-like objects slowly moving down the street in a flanking formation. Near the front were strange-looking vehicles, white trucks that seemed to sit on rotary brushes. The front end sleeked down to form a beak like that of a giant toucan. Charlie watched as the machines squirted water on the streets while the brushes scrubbed. The action created a wave that, by 8:43, seemed to be shooting the street's trash along the curb.

There were a few minutes of silence before Charlie heard a new and different noise, a rather grating, scraping sound. Charlie spied from his window and smiled as he thought to himself that the foot soldiers had arrived. They were a curious army of men and women tightly bundled against the now chilly February night air. Their weapons were shovels which were used to scoop the soggy trash from the curb wall into plastic bags.

It was now 9:12, and the action was switching to another front. "The lancers have arrived," Charlie laughed to himself. Indeed, a platoon of men were marching along the neutral ground, their path illuminated by the yellow haze from the city lights. Their weapons were spears, sticks with a spike at one end, with which they impaled bits of wayward litter. With each plunge, the men lifted their booty into plastic bags. As their march continued in the direction of the now-distant parade, they left behind huge sacks stuffed with riches of their plunder.

By then it was 10:20, and again there was silence except for both the sweeping sound outside made by the last wave of the sidewalk broom brigade and the rustling noise of dried leaves fluttering in chilled wind. Those sounds allowed tranquility enough for Charlie to lapse into his nightly doze.

But at 10:43, that sleep was interrupted by the rapid-fire sound of men shouting. Charlie rushed to his window, where he spotted a sanitation truck rolling cautiously along the street. Like pirates collecting their contraband, men were running on either side, lifting the waiting bags of trash and tossing them into the truck bed.

That disturbance caused Charlie to notice that it was almost time for the shift change, his quitting time. Charlie made his final inspection of the building and then stepped outside for the first time that evening. The street was now without liter and shining from its cleaning. It looked better than it did on normal nights. The neutral ground was cleaner than when he had arrived at work that day, at an hour when the letting out of the nearby school had triggered the first assault on the green space. It was 11:00, and at that moment, his little world seemed as miraculously clean as the air felt brisk. The silence was broken only by the swish of tires on the hosed-down street.

As Charlie walked toward the bus stop, he thought about his evening. Usually the nights on the job were uninteresting and lonely. But on this night during the Carnival season, he had witnessed from his window precision movement and orchestration — a spectacular only-in-New Orleans show. He thought how impressed he was by what he had seen, and then he thought to add — he had enjoyed the parade, too.

Easy Rider

It was 1969, the year when Hollywood would send two motor-cyclists, named Captain America and Billy, across the nation's movie screens and in the process have a serious effect on New Orleans' Mardi Gras.

Easy Rider was the film, a tale about the counter-culture generation, a group to whom the only champions were antiheroes. Captain and Billy (played by Peter Fonda and Dennis Hopper), won such adulation as they set out to discover America and, in the process, found Mardi Gras.

Much of the story was about the hardships that the cyclist encountered in their not-so-easy ride. The tour became a farce as they reached rural Louisiana, where drawling rednecks snarled about the length of their hair. But New Orleans, ah, New Orleans — the city was Babylon in this cultural desert. The town, as Captain and Billy saw it, was dreamy but seedy, which was the way, of course, that anti-heroes and their followers liked it. The two found love, highs, music and, most of all, tolerance amidst the maskers and paraders seemingly floating through the Quarter.

Cities beg to be depicted favorably in movies, as New Orleans was in this film, at least in the eyes of that particular audience. But the city paid a price. *Easy Rider* became a cult film and Mardi Gras became the cult's big event. For the next few years, thousands of make-believe Captain Americas and Billys came in search of truth and goodness. They came with free spirits and budgets to match. They crowded the streets, slept on the steps; some begged for food while others were too stoned to ask. There was outrage in a community which was, during that time period when "relevance" was a buzzword, already chastising itself over questions of Carnival's social and economic implications. Mardi Gras was in trouble.

It should be noted that ultimately the city responded with some of the tolerance with which the movie had credited it. There was little back-woods justice, rather an orderly attempt to deal with the problems. Tulane University students founded the Mardi Gras Coalition to deal with the medical and legal problems of visitors. The university provided sleeping space in its stadium. The police became masters at gentle but firm persuasion in enforcing the loitering laws. And the city spread the word to the nation's counter-culture presses that the self-proclaimed Greatest Free Show on Earth has a cost.

Within a few years the problem no longer existed, partially because of the city's effort, but more because the days of the Easy Rider generation had ended. The kids had grown, and the film was nostalgia to be viewed at art theatres on nights when a babysitter was available.

If Captain America and Billy could somehow visit New Orleans again they would see a city that has changed in the 16 years that they have aged. The Roosevelt Hotel, which they danced past, has been renamed the Fairmont and is now joined by a line of other grand hotels at which those of their generation now stay, some on expense accounts. They might also notice a change in the character of Carnival, too, because it happened that in 1969, the same year of *Easy Rider's* release, there was another event which would revive the festival.

That was the year the Krewe of Bacchus started as an attempt to spark Carnival with the energy of bigness, both in the size of its floats and in the names of celebrities. Other krewes would follow.

As they walk the city's streets, Captain and Billy may or may not find the magic they experienced nearly two decades earlier, but that may be a reflection more on differences in their lives than in Carnival's condition. Sometimes the changes in Carnival must be measured not as much by the size of its floats as in the spirit of its people.

THE IRISH

Parasol's

Assessor Ronnie Burke was working the crowd at Parasol's bar and restaurant on Constance Street. Showing remarkable wrist action, his right hand moved from one clasp to another as he made the round of the tables.

Burke wasn't seeking votes because he had just been re-elected and the totals of his landslide left nothing to fear. He was probably pumping hands because his name is Burke, he lives in the Irish Channel and it's near St. Patrick's Day, and he happened to be in Parasol's so that was the thing to do. It's what his father, the late assessor, used to do. That's the Irish way.

This is the time of year for trekking to Parasol's. The pub is the unofficial cradle of the local Irish civilization, the place where they meet on St. Paddy's Day to drink green beer and toast the old country that many of them have never seen. Parasol's is the Shamrock of Ages for generations of loyal Irish.

Until recently, I had never been to Parasol's, but with St. Pat's feast approaching it seemed like the right place for a quick lunch while absorbing a bit of local color. I've eaten there three times now, which hardly makes me a regular but at least allows me to want to conclude that, like the Irish Channel, Parasol's is something different from its popular image.

There are trappings of Irish appreciation. A sign above the bar hawks Irish walking sticks ($35) for the big parade. Along the walls are various proclamations and articles about the antics of these committed disciples of St. Paddy. In the dining room, another sign advertises "Kiss Me I'm Irish" buttons. And, during my second visit, the Canadian Club salesman stopped by to drop off various St. Patrick's Day promotional items which now decorate the place.

But through it all, another culture is pervasive. Try as they might, Parasol's isn't Irish as much as it is Noo Awlins. It's not cabbage or stew that causes crowds in the dining room but poor boys, some with fried oysters, others dripping with roast beef. The bartender doesn't pour whiskey as often as he serves Barq's and Dixie. Except for the one that says Notre Dame, the pennants on the wall don't have anything to do with the Irish but plenty to do with football. And while there might be a certain amount of blarney in the bar room conversation, the tone is hometown blue collar.

Down the row, an elderly man wants attention. "Did you get the tip I left you last Friday?" the man asks the bartender. "No," the tender replies, seeming a bit annoyed by the topic. "Well, I left you a tip," the old man assures, "but you know I don't have to leave tips anymore, I'm on Social Security now." The old man laughs, the bartender doesn't.

"Gimme a large oyster dressed," a customer demands. "Tulane and LSU are going to play each other on TV Friday night," someone at the far end of the bar announces while thumbing through the newpaper.

Had there been a native Irishman listening to the conversation he may not have gotten past trying to imagine what a large oyster looks like when it's dressed. The folks at Parasol's have no such problem, because they all speak native talk.

Nevertheless, they'll be thinking Irish at Parasol's on St. Patrick's Day and they'll be singing along with the old songs from the jukebox. Environments may change and people assimilate, but some traditions survive. Parasol's is a shamrock in a field of azaleas. 'Tis the luck of the Irish that the clover is a sturdy plant.

March Of The Irish

There are certain informal rules that a person should be aware of when experiencing the St. Patrick's Day parade in the Irish Channel.

Rule One is to begin by going to the corner of Third and Constance Streets and joining the crowd waiting outside of Parasol's bar for the parade to begin. While waiting, those in the crowd sort of mill about looking for beer and friendly faces — some of which are painted with shamrocks.

At some point it is appropriate to ask if anyone has seen the parade, which brings up the second rule: be aware that, although a few hundred people are waiting at that corner, the parade's route is actually a block away. In fact, you should also be aware (Rule Three) that many of those people are concerned only with being near the bar at Parasol's and don't really care about the parade.

Rule Four begins after you have walked to Magazine Street to see the parade. The rule states simply that he who stands in one spot to wait for the Irish Channel parade to completely pass may still be standing in that spot when the Rose parade is rolling in Pasadena in January. There are many wonderful things to be said about the Irish and their parades, but neither can be noted for their speed during the St. Patrick's procession. The groups are disjointed and there are many delays, probably because someone has stopped for a quick trip to Parasol's. Whatever the reason, it is far better to walk up alongside the parade. It's a new concept in parade watching — the crowd marches past the parade rather than waiting for the parade to pass it.

Some people who ride in the parade, like Judge Robert Katz and Councilman Jim Singleton, don't look very Irish, but don't be fooled by that. Rule Five cautions that in the Channel, Irishness is a state of mind. Where else can you find shamrocks in Latin bars?

Nor (this is Rule Six) is the spirit limited just to humans. One of the units in the parade was a group of people walking their dogs under the banner of the Deep South Irish Wolfhounds Club.

Rule Seven should not be taken lightly: Be alert to the trucks and floats in the parade. Getting stung by beads or doubloons is one thing but it's quite another experience to be hit by an errant potato or cabbage. Besides going fishing, a St. Patrick's Day parade is the only other experience I know of where a person can catch supper. Like fishing, catching the greens (Rule Eight) is apparently a skill sport that knows no class boundaries. I saw a former Rex walking home with a booty of cabbage and shallots.

Beer, green or otherwise, is the basis of Rule Nine, which preaches that purveyors of such should be sure that they're well supplied. By contrast, Parasol's ran out of the suds by mid-afternoon on the day of the parade, which is equivalent to Wendy's running out of beef. In fact, the rest of the afternoon on the corner of Constance and Third might have been a disaster had it not been for various marching groups and trucks that had completed the parade route and begun their own independent marches which worked their way through the crowds alongside Parasol's. As one of these groups, the Zig-Zag Jazz Band, marched by, there was suddenly gyrating and hand clapping in the crowd, thereby proving Rule Ten, which is true in life as well as on St. Patrick's Day in the Channel: A parade will always find you, if you only know how to find the right spot.

Irish On Parade

At around 8:30 in the evening, give or take a half hour or so, the lead unit of the Decatur Street St. Patrick's Day Parade turned from Madison Street in the Quarter onto Decatur as the procession began the last few blocks of its march. A crowd estimated by authorities to be in the tens of thousands waited anxiously to experience the ritual of Ireland's patron being honored. This is what they saw:

At about 8:35, give or take a few minutes, the Marine Band, which had grown weary of waiting for the rest of the parade to catch up, stepped off to its rendition of that beloved Irish hymn, "The Halls of Montezuma."

Close behind was a decorated truck carrying the membership of a somber group known as, "Lynn's Irish Cultural Society & Just Plain Drunks." One Irishman on the truck grasped a female fellow passenger on the shoulder while shouting to the bystanders, "This is Lynn." Whether Lynn belonged to the cultural faction or the drunk faction of the group was undetermined.

What can better capture the spirit of old Ireland than a Scottish bagpipe band playing "When the Saints Go Marching In?" That's what followed.

By then, the music was flowing. After the melodies of the bagpipes those along Decatur were treated to the harmonics of a loudspeaker in one of Criminal Sheriff Charles Foti's squad cars. The selection for that segment of the parade was from one of the Emerald Isle's favorite groups, James Brown and the Fabulous Flames. In keeping with an old

Irish custom, fuzzy Pac Men dangled from the squad car's rear view mirror.

Irishmen, of course, are always prepared, which explains why the next unit was a 1954 fire truck belonging to something called the Overpeck Fire Department. In case anyone along the way had a flame they needed extinguished, a sign on the truck side assured that the vehicle was for rent.

A cluster of men in tuxedos carrying paper carnations straggled along next. They handed the flowers to women along the route in exchange for kisses. One marcher had even refined his approach, charming the females by singing out as he walked along, "I've got herpes tonight."

A limousine followed, the kind with the shaded windows so that mere mortals on the outside can't see in. The sign on the side said merely "Molly Men." But just so the grim limo would not dampen spirits, the next unit was no doubt provided to provoke a few chuckles — an official car from the coroner's office.

Next came the Krewe of Joe's Jungle Marching Club, followed by a service vehicle for the krewe. The vehicle, a flatbed truck, contained the two essentials for every successful marching group: a keg and a portable outhouse. A woman in green stood in front of the outhouse door, waving to the crowd, while not noticing that she was preventing an Irishman within from being able to open the door.

Another limousine followed, this one carrying men in tuxedos with no announced purpose in particular. One stood in the opening of the sunroof, concocting an old Irish recipe consisting of Michelob poured into a Hurricane glass.

Three men straggled along, each wearing a T-shirt announcing, "I-Rish I were on Decatur Street."

Thirty-five miscellaneous Irishmen weaved by.

A Metairie group, the Cleary Marching Club, dressed in Fat City white, weaved along the path.

A mule-drawn carriage followed, which may or may not have been part of the parade.

Finally, the blinking lights from another sheriff's squad car signaled that the parade had ended.

Across the street at Tujague's, customers went back to their boiled beef dinners. One band that had lost its way marched towards Jackson Square.

Meanwhile, the marchers had reached their starting and ending point, Molly's at the Market restaurant. There would be street music and beer. The man in the outhouse was finally able to free himself. He, along with his fellow Irishmen, knew that now that the serious business of the parade was over, it was time to party.

FIGS

This has been a figless summer, although friends have tried to help. A few have delivered plastic bags filled with figs right off the tree. They've also brought Mason jars stuffed with some of their syrupy homemade preserves. One even embellished her fig preserves with ginger, creating a taste which is better than when I cook my own. Still, fig season hasn't been the same — not since my tree died.

That tree had its day. In its prime, it flourished with more than 1,000 figs per summer. It was like a semi-tropical Christmas tree resplendent with tiny ornaments. The birds would snatch a few; a few were out of reach, and some splattered the neighbors' yard. But that still left plenty for picking.

Then one autumn, as the leaves were starting to drop, the trunk split vertically, causing one of the arms to fall. There were only a few figs the following summer. The tree was dying as vines, like buzzards, began to circle the trunk. An axe brought to an end what must have been decades of summertime glory.

Those fig tree umbrellas sprout throughout New Orleans as though to protect yards from the summer heat and rain. In fact, figs are probably the most plentiful edibles grown within the city's boundaries.

Still, it's hard to take figs seriously. Just the word sounds funny. "What are you writing your column about this week?" a fellow worker asked me. "Figs," I said. "Figs!" she retorted while walking away laughing. She would have probably laughed harder if I had told her that, to me, figs are the consummate urban fruit. They grow in bundles, especially in steamy climates such as New Orleans'. They can be eaten raw, right off the branch, or they can be preserved and saved forever, or at least until a winter morning when they are served with hot biscuits.

Somehow, the big-payoff-for-little-effort character of figs fits the something-for-nothing ethos of the city. Figs and New Orleans belong together. But there is a certain physical price to be paid for having your figs and eating them too. There's a stickiness to the fig leaves that has left an occasional temporary itch on generations of fig pickers. Then nature plays a rather pixyish timing trick. It happens that figs ripen in early July, at the beginning of the hottest time of the year. That's all right, unless someone wants to preserve the crop. Watching over and stirring a pot of boiling figgy syrup is a hot job.

Then the jars and their lids have to be sterilized by boiling, at least for those of us who are finicky. Finally, there's the penance of standing in a hot kitchen on a hot July day, spooning hot fig preserves into hot jars and then twisting on hot lids. As they say in City Hall, "There's no such thing as a free lunch."

But it's a price worth paying. I'm pleased to report that a young fig tree now grows near where the older one stood. It was planted two years ago and has somehow survived my agricultural philosophy, which was patterned after the teachings of Adam Smith and Charles Darwin — laissez faire and survival of the fittest. The little tree is bright with green leaves these days and looks like a tot trying to dress in an adult's clothes. It has also shown its first sign of maturity. Last week the tree yielded the first of its fruit. I stood in the area of where I once gathered figs by the hundreds to pick one solitary fig - a lonely harbinger of a new generation.

It wasn't much of a crop, but to a fig picker without figs to pick, it at least provided hope that there won't be another figless summer.

A Sequel

This hasn't been a figless summer after all. Sure, the untimely death of my fig tree left me without a crop to preserve; but ever since the demise was reported in this column recently the response has kept alive the memory of happier days around the fig tree.

It turns out that there are lots of fig fans out there, some of whom used the occasion to write so that they could console me and tell of their experiences. One person wrote, "My 82-year-old grandmother and I share your preoccupation with figs. She has a huge tree which she religiously climbs into every year (orthopedic shoes and all) to reap her crop.

"All year long," the letter continues, "we anticipate this delectable July feast. Throughout the year we inspect the tree for new growth, feed and water it for a sweeter crop, and plant cuttings just in case, God forbid, our tree dies. By early April we predict the condition of the year's crop. And what sweet ambrosia it is!"

Another person wrote to say that the column "brought tears to my eyes when it reminded me of the multi-branched tree in my parents' backyard. My imagination and I took many trips on countless climbs (including onto the corrugated tin roof of our garage — a mother's nightmare)."

That latter letter brought up a good point. It's true, fig trees seem to always be found around tin sheds or garages. It may have been part of the natural order of things to allow fig pickers fig picking platforms, but if 82- year-old grandmothers (orthopedic shoes and all) are actually climbing the trees, the shed may be in danger of extinction. Did you ever notice that you're seeing more spritely grandmothers around these days and fewer tin sheds with corrugated roofs?

Regardless of their location, all trees sooner or later must meet the grim fig reaper. "Our tree split and passed away also," one person wrote. "But fortunately, my sister, who is probably more sentimental than I, has grown a fig tree in her backyard from a cutting of our childhood tree. Two and a half years ago she gave me a fledgling fig tree which was, in turn, grown from a cutting of her tree."

That letter set the tone of things, as was made explicit in the first letter, the one from the person with the tree-climbing grandmother. After telling of a near fatality when a branch of their tree died, the letter writer concluded: "The moral of this story is always have a sapling to plant, just in case. You can always give it away when it gets too big. I have an extra sapling and so does my grandmother. Do this and you'll never have a figless summer again."

All the hubbub, incidentally, seems to justify the thesis of my original column and that is that figs are the ultimate urban fruit and that they deserve more recognition. Surprisingly, that recognition has been slow in coming, even in a city like New Orleans with a repuatation for food and festivity. Only the Italians, who save their fig preserves until March, when they are used for cuccidattas (fig cookies) or pastries in honor of St. Joseph and St. Lucia, have taken full advantage of the fig. The outrageousness of this oversight has even hit close to home with the revelation that the Gambit cookie fund has favored chocolate chips and systematically ignored Fig Newtons.

Meanwhile, fig picking season has ended. Only unripened tiny green bulbs remain beneath the large leaves. The leaves gradually brown and then fall. But from the letters it's obvious that figs have loyal fans and that many pantry shelves are now stocked to assure that there won't be a figless winter, either.

Figs: The Second Year

A few months ago I was on a panel at Mount Carmel High School where, for an hour or so, a former teacher and I answered questions and talked about the economy, crime, the press and politics. At the end of the period a student raised her hand to ask one last question. Are you going to write another column about figs this year? she asked.

Yes, Virginia, there will be another column on figs, and this is it. A year has passed since this space accidentally discovered what legions of fig fans there are out there.

On the fig front this year it can be reported, at least from a personal perspective, that the little tree in the backyard, the one that took the place of the old one, has grown a bit more and has produced some figs, but hardly enough to fill much more than a couple of Fig Newtons.

It will obviously still be a few years before the tree will be producing a supply equal to its predecessor, so this year I've had to stay in stock as a freelance fig picker.

My services were rendered at the home of friends who have three redwood-size trees growing together in a clump, which brings up the topic of scaling the fig tree. Ladders, of course, are handy but that's kind of like using a shotgun to hunt a butterfly. Fair play in stalking the wild fig requires actually making way through the leaves and twigs and climbing the tree. A real fig picker leaves the fruit on the lower bottom edges of the tree to the women and children, for the true adventure rests near the top.

There is no fig quite like a hard-to-get fig. . . the one that crowns the tree. It isn't necessarily bigger or better than any other fig, it's just that it's there. Reaching that fig sometimes requires risking not only life but occasionally limb — if not yours, the tree's.

What adds to the suspense is that the figs that are hardest for humans to reach, the ones nearest the top, are also the ones that are easiest for birds to attack. Just like the adventurer who, in finally reaching the lost mine, discovers that it has been plundered by thieves, the illusive fig is sometimes spoiled by pockmarks from wayward birds. No one said that life was always going to be fair.

Even those who finally grab the fig of their desire still have the problem of what to do with it. While clutching to a bowing limb it is not always easy to be gentle in handling a fragile fig. One answer is to carry a small bowl but that tends to tip over during the climb. Another solution is to gently lob the fig to a compatriot down at ground level. Then there's a final solution which is to eat the fig. It's a convenient alternative but one that leaves you with no trophy to show for your efforts.

Something that is left from combat with the tree is the sticky feeling that comes from the white "milk" in the leaves. It is the tree's revenge, a way of getting back at you for violating its space. But it's a mild revenge, one that is easily gotten rid of with soap and water, worth the trouble considering the spoils to be eaten.

There's a Ziploc bag filled with top-of-the-tree figs in my refrigerator now. But as I peel the cold figs I look out at the little tree in the backyard and remember better days when the supply was bountiful and the pot on the stove was filled with fig preserves. Those days will return after the tree reaches manhood. Until then there are the adventures of freelance fig picking to live with, and memories of the ones that got away.

THE HANSENS

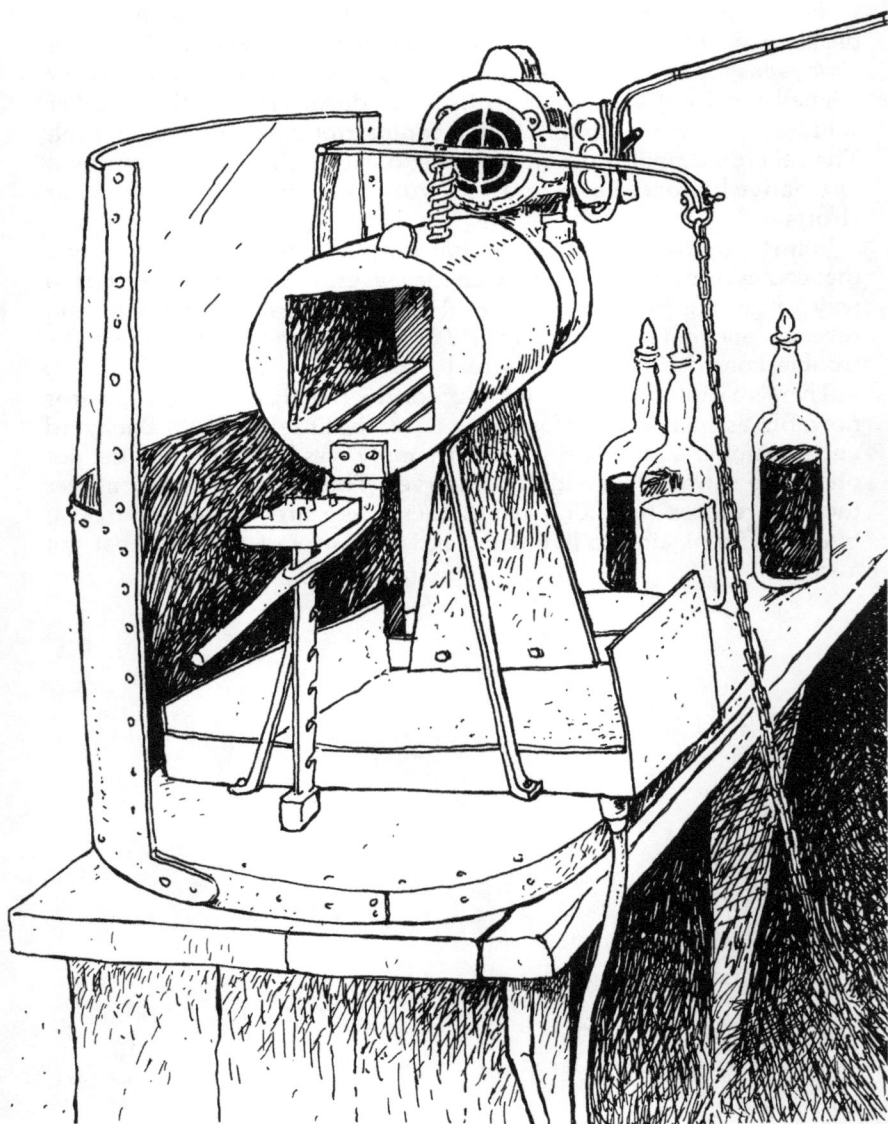

Snow Business

There's a gallery in the French Quarter that displays a drawing showing a kindly looking couple preparing a snowball. The man in the sketch is operating a barrelish looking machine while his wife applies the fixings.

That print comes to life each day except Saturday, between spring and fall, when Ernest and Mary Hansen reach for the ice at Hansen's Sno-Bliz Sweet Shop.

If ever there was a mom-and-pop operation that should be destined not only for an artist's print but for a spot in the Presbytere, it is the Hansen's snowball stand. For over 45 years now, Ernest Hansen has been pulling the lever on the snowball machine that he invented while wife Mary has been shaking on her home concocted flavors. Quite simply, Hansen's Sweet Shop is the world's greatest snowball stand.

I make that claim without timidity because no other snowball outlet has all that Hansen's has. For one, there is the machine itself. Other places buy their ice machines, but Ernest Hansen's is the one and only. There is no other. It shows ice no mercy, leaving a fine powdery snow that would shame nature. Then there is Mary Hansen's syrups — rich blends combining extracts softened with spring water (never tap water) and then mixed with a velvety cream.

There's also the sense of marketing. Those are not ordinary snowballs that the Hansens serve. There is the standard fare, but for $6 a customer can invest in a Superdome shaped snowball that could probably feed the Saints. Buy a Superdome and Mrs. Hansen also snaps your picture.

But the domes are among the more modest purchases. As I sat in Mrs. Hansen's back kitchen she was finishing a special order — four two gallon buckets of snowball. Price: $25 apiece. It was for a good cause, though. The air conditioner was broken at the Civil Courts building so a sympathetic law firm had bought a bucket of snowball for the workers on each floor of the building. Justice is rendered in different ways.

In addition to it all, Hansen's is special because of the ambiance. At a time when people of lesser will would have fled to the suburbs, the Hansens are still at the same location, right on the corner of the 2800 block of Tchoupitoulas, in the shadow of passing ships and across from the Public Belt Railroad. The neighborhood has had its ups and downs, but then Hansen's really isn't just a neighborhood snowball stand. It has a regional following, as attested to by the newspaper and magazine articles that decorate one wall. The artist knew what he was doing. If ever there was a scene that captures an idyllic image of everyday New Orleans it is the Hansens serving the line of customers that sometimes stretches down the block.

How big is their business? They sell Hansen's Sno Bliz T-shirts, caps and cups.

How big is their business? "You know I didn't even know about that drawing until someone gave a copy to my son as a present," Mary Hansen recalls. "A lot of people come here and take pictures, I guess the artist just came in one day, took a picture, and did a drawing from that. I hear it's selling for $175. I wish. . . "

Suddenly the conversation is interrupted by the appearance of a small girl in the doorway of the back kitchen. The girl stares shyly up at Mrs. Hansen. "What do you want, sweetheart?" Mary Hansen asks. The little girl merely stares. Finally, Ernest Hansen leaves the ice machine for an instant to tell his wife that the girl needs to go to the bathroom.

Through a door, into the supply room towards another door, Mary Hansen and the little girl walk. No matter how big they get, sometimes a mom and pop can't help just being a mom and pop.

Tchoupitoulas And Bordeaux

Her brood was about to undergo one of the first rites of being a New Orleanian. From the rapid fire of questions aimed at her from the seven children at her ankles, her name obviously was Charlene, a women in her thirties who had undertaken the formidable challenge of taking this gang for snowballs.

To Charlene's credit, these were not just any snowballs but the best there are, the world's greatest snowballs, served at Hansen's on the corner of Tchoupitoulas and Bordeaux streets in the city that made the true "snowball," as opposed to the Yankee "sno-cone," famous.

Charlene assigned the seven toddlers to sit on the metal bench outside, while she stood in the inevitable line stretching from the door into the storefront building to the counter, where Ma and Pa Hansen have begun their 43rd summer of making the quintessential snowball.

As they sat impatiently, the seven were no doubt unaware of what made the snowball which they were about to receive so special. Perhaps one day they could appreciate Mr. Hansen's homemade barrel-like ice machine — the only one of its kind, creating a snow better than nature's and far finer than the commercial machines all other snowball stands must use. They might also appreciate the syrups, made in the back kitchen by Momma Hansen. Her tart flavors alone, lemonade and orange, will land her into the Snowball Hall of Fame.

Add to that the charm not only of the Hansens, but of a business that has stood its ground on Tchoupitoulas Street for five decades, and the result is a New Orleans classic.

But none of that would mean anything to the kids, who had grown so restless that they had begun screaming out their names, giggling all along while being affected by anything that entered their sight. "My name's Tyrone Anthony Jones," one shouted. "My name's Truck," another giggled. "My name's Garbage Can," a third laughed harder. The teenager who had been assigned by Charlene to watch over the group sought discipline by reaching for the pay phone and feigning to call the police, perhaps on a charge of giving false testimony outside a snowball stand. "But you have to dial 911," one tyke explained obviously having seen this ploy before.

Meanwhile Charlene, having heard the commotion, appeared and announced angrily that if she had to leave her place in line once more there would be no snowballs. That was a serious threat, as those who formed the growing line could give tribute to. Newspaper clippings on the inside wall tell of Hansen's regional popularity. A citation from MENU magazine gives it a three-star rating, undeniably the highest rating ever given in gourmet circles to a snowball dispensary. And various plaques and citations reveal the place as being a favorite haunt for fraternities.

But perhaps the best tribute came from Charlene's gang, the members of which sat more or less quietly in the face of a threatened snowball embargo. Quiet, until Charlene reappeared with the first of the snowballs. "These two are for the little children," Charlene announced. "I'm little," one of the older ones shouted, showing no pride but admirable cunning in immediate pursuit of a genuine Hansens. One day when they are older they might be able to take advantage of Hansen's innovation for 1986, take-out service for her "Frozens" -an iced snowball of sorts with ice cream in the center, "People would complain that they would have to wait in line for two hours to get these," Mary Hansen explained while husband Ernest reloaded his machine with ice. "Now they can just come in and pick them up." With success comes innovation.   Success was being played out outside as well as Charlene dispensed the rest of the snowballs. She had performed her duties well and had rewarded herself by getting a snowball with a twist of whipped cream on top.   She might have gotten to enjoy this luxury had not one of the group spotted the white crown and begged for a dash on top of his snowball. The others fell in line as Charlene grudgingly spooned bits from her snowball onto the assembly line below. As Charlene and her gang walked away, she may have realized that the only problem with eating something so good is that sometimes you just have to share.

The First

I drove hurriedly up Napoleon Avenue, hoping I could get there in time for the opening at 3:00 p.m. But this was more than an effort to be there in time to tell the story; this year I had a shot at being part of that story. This could be my year to be number one.

Two years ago I had tried to be first, but an over-anxious Tulane med student edged me out. I had to settle for second place. Last year I missed the opening completely. So I had had two years of waiting for this moment.

I turned right on Tchoupitoulas and glanced nervously at my watch. It was four minutes to opening. Might I have to settle for second place again? By then I could spot the familiar landmarks. There on the river side was the Public Belt Railroad's building and on the other side was the little white building where I might have a rendezvous with history. As I pulled alongside I glanced again at my watch. It was 15 seconds to three. Then I noticed that six people had arrived there before me, standing there waiting.

By rights I should have been upset at that point. Despite my efforts, I could have finished no higher than seventh place, but I also knew that I had one advantage, the deck was stacked in my favor. Mr. Hansen was standing outside. As he saw me approach he waved me to the front door. "We'll open in just a few minutes," Hansen told the waiting customers.

Soon I was inside the home of the world's greatest snowball stand, Hansen's Sno Bliz. Ernest and Mary Hansen were this afternoon opening their shop for the forty-somethingth year. "We remember when you were second two years ago," Mrs. Hansen said, "so we wanted to be sure you were first this year." Outside, two Tulane coeds were tapping on the window wanting to get in. Sure, this was rigged to my advantage, but I had paid my dues suffering the heartbreak of the runner-up spot.

Mary Hansen told how she had been there the night before until 2:00 a.m. preparing her flavors. She showed the design for a new cup to be introduced this year that has an illustration of the couple on it. They are pictured alongside the snow machine that Ernest Hansen invented nearly five decades ago. It is a one-and-only that makes the finest snow this side of the Rockies.

But the tapping was getting louder. It was time to get down to business. Between that moment and next October the Hansens will serve up thousands of snowballs, but I had the responsibility of deciding on the first one. In baseball the first pitch of the season might be a high fastball, the first hit a double to left. I can report for the history books that the first Hansen snowball of the 1983 season was a dollar-sized combination creme of nectar and creme of chocolate.

Meanwhile, the window thumping was intense. Some people just have no appreciation for ceremony. Mary Hansen, who was in her little kitchen in the back busily mixing syrups asked me if I would open the door. Not only was I the opening day pitcher, I was also the usher unlocking the gates.

While the line formed, Ernest Hansen was busy preparing my snowball. Like a true craftsman he worked carefully, meticulously following the proper procedures. A layer of ice, a splash of nectar, more ice, some chocolate, still more ice, then chocolate on one side and nectar on the other. There it was, the first snowball of the season.

I was ready to dig into it, but there was still one bit of ceremony left. Mr. Hansen pulled out his Polaroid. Picture taking is common at Hansen's, as is evident by the snapshots that decorate the place. When you're number one you have to accept the flashing lights. In the spirit of good sportsmanship, Mrs. Hansen urged the two girls, whose snowballs would be numbers two and three, to join in the picture. There we stood, smiling, the triumvirate of the '83 season.

While we posed, a strange phenomenon was taking place. There is a mystery of the riverfront that happens every year on opening day. Somehow, when the Hansens open their door, word spreads throughout uptown New Orleans as though an alarm were attached to the hinges. Within moments, 12 additional people were in line. Then a police car rushed to the scene. Three parched looking cops walked in. "Hi, Mrs. Hansen," one said, "Boy, we've been waiting for you to open."

By this time the two girls had their snowballs. One pointed to the spot on the wall where an earlier snapshot of her stood. "You'll have to bring the fellas in before they go home for the summer," Mary Hansen advised the girl.

By now the line had extended out the door. The two girls were searching the walls for snapshots of friends from Tulane. Mary Hansen was again in the back stirring her syrups. Ernest Hansen was making snow with his machines. The season was in full swing; I quietly finished my snowball and left. Everyone was busy. It's true what they say, it is lonely at the top.

MR. BINGLE

Who Shot Mr. Bingle

Back in the 1950s, Mr. Bingle became one of the first stars of New Orleans television. Maison Blanche's little snowman marionette had his own show each evening during the Christmas season. He would prance about while wearing his ice cream cone hat and waving his peppermint cane. Bingle's holly wings also allowed him to float over the set.

As he pranced, waved, and floated, Bingle reminded all the kids out there about the toys available at MB. The fact that the snowman's initials were the same as the department store's was lost to those of us who were more concerned with the bounty than the retailer. People to whom Santa Claus is plausible don't pay much attention to marketing strategies.

Nevertheless, part of that strategy included a nifty little jingle (the Bingle jingle?) that introduced the show. It lingers:

Jingle, jangle, jingle
Here comes Mr. Bingle
With another message from Kris Kringle
Time to launch the Christmas season
Maison Blanche makes Christmas pleasin'
Gifts galore for you to see
Each a gem from MB.

Inevitably, the sweet little darlings of New Orleans created a shortened schoolyard version of the song:

Jingle, jangle, jingle
Who shot Mr. Bingle
With a bullet from Kris Kringle. . .

I found myself mumbling the latter version last week, after news that the Maison Blanche chain had been sold to Goudchaux's of Baton Rouge but the new owners would not operate the downtown store. The economic significance of the announcement is in itself subject for pondering. But what I'm concerned about is the future of Mr. Bingle.

When the department store's high rollers worked out this deal, Bingle was obviously a bargaining chip. The press announcement made a point of mentioning that the purchasers would also recieve the rights to the snowman. What this means is that Mr. Bingle is leaving downtown. It is the ultimate urban insult: snow white flight.

No longer will he perform in MB's display window along Canal Street. No longer will the gargantuan Bingle decorate the top of the store, like an angel crested on a Christmas tree, from Thanksgiving to New Year's Day. Instead, Bingle is moving to the suburbs, working regional shopping centers, entertaining the kiddies sequestered in nowhere land.

All of this has left me with a sense of not only loss but lost opportunity. I will not how have the chance to do that special column I had been keeping for one day. In it, I would hypothesize an interview with the snowman during the off-season. In my version, Bingle would be a committed urban dweller spending the other 11 months living in a renovated shotgun ice box somewhere near Hansen's Snow Bliz shop on Tchoupitoulas Street.

We would have begun by talking about old times, like the evening when he danced too near a footlight on the television set and the children of New Orleans got to watch Bingle's crotch smolder — live.

We'd talk about new directions in his career. . . like last year when MB ran a Christmas time ad pushing children's underwear. Right on top was tiny Bingle wearing red jockey shorts.

Were you trying for a new image, Bingle?

Would you do a "Cosmopolitan" centerfold?

Why red?

I could, of course, still interview Bingle as a suburbanite, catching him creeping along the interstate or polishing his sleigh in his driveway, but it just won't be the same. As far as I'm concerned, Mr. Bingle joins the Falstaff weather ball and K&B nectar sodas as another part of lost New Orleans.

On the morning of Sunday, January 3, 1982 there was a traffic stall along the 900 block of Canal Street. Police were directing the passing automobiles into one lane to make room for the huge trucks in front of Maison Blanche. Eyes gazed upward. The giant Bingle atop Maison Blanche was being lowered by a crane. The same procedure had been followed each year. It seemed like it was just part of the annual ritual of closing down the Christmas season. We didn't realize at the time that we were witnessing the end of an institution and the beginning of a memory. Somehow, memories seem to be becoming more plentiful.

Bingle Explained

Dear Streetcar,

I'm new to town and I've got a question. What is all the ruckus among locals about this character Mr. Bingle? A few weeks ago this huge figure of him was placed on the front of the Maison Blanche Building and the press reacted to it as though an oil well had been discovered in City Hall's front lawn. Now as I walk through the department stores there are dolls of him all over the place and signs announcing personal appearances. I don't understand. He just seems to me like a sissy overgrown marshmallow with a squeaky voice. What's the big deal?
—*Virginia.*

Yes, Virginia, they do make a big deal out of Mr. Bingle here, perhaps even more than you realize. Did you know, for example, that several years ago when the Maison Blanche (in case you haven't caught on yet, Mr. Bingle's initials are the same as the department store he represents) chain was sold, that a good bit of the negotiations, and the press coverage thereof, were over the use of the name and rights to Bingle? Mr. Bingle was part of the deal in the sale. That squeaky voice squeaks loudly.

Anyway, in answer to your question I can think of two reasons for his popularity. One is that he is the only symbol of Christmas that is unique to New Orleans. Look at the other symbols — one-horse open sleighs dashing through the snow, Victorian table settings, wise men in the East — none of those have anything to do with life in New Orleans. But Bingle, he's one of our guys. He was born and raised in New Orleans and will no doubt always live here. This year, his positioning on the Maison Blanche building meant more than just the coming of Christmas, it was an indication of the possible renaissance of the downtown area. Bingle was missing from that spot for a couple of years after the store's original owners moved out of the building. It was more than just child's play that the big Bingle was gone — it was a sign that the business district might be in trouble, a sign merely underscored by the absence of a seasonal landmark.

Bingle can fly, but he's no magician. His return doesn't guarantee downtown's success but it is at least encouraging that he is back smiling from his traditional perch and not just working suburban shopping centers. In the right context, even a silly flying snowman can have meaning.

As for the other reason, I think it has more to do with just the sort of corny old nostalgia around which Christmas is made. There's a whole generation of people out there, who are now in their professional prime, who remember Bingle on television when they were kids. They've changed, the city has changed, but Bingle still looks and talks the same. To that group, the first television generation, Mr. Bingle was one of the first public characters in their lives. He was a local Big Bird in a snow suit.

Bingle doesn't do much television anymore, even though he was an industry pioneer. Instead, he seems to be concentrating more on appearances at department stores where another generation is learning about and will no doubt one day appreciate New Orleans' one and only Christmas character.

I do agree with your basic criticism, Virginia. I can see where to someone not raised with him, Mr. Bingle is not much to look at or listen to. I cannot recall one memorable quote from his button mouth or a great thought from beneath his ice cream cone cap. He's a rather bland, powerless character made lovable only because he's been around and we've known him all our lives. But doesn't there seem to be something Christmas-like in that?

Oscar

Oscar Isentrout was one of those interviews that got away. When I last saw him he was having lunch in a downtown restaurant. Seeing him reminded me that I should try to interview him soon. It wasn't soon enough; he died last week at 61.

His full name was Edwin Harmon Oscar Isentrout, but he was better recognized for being the voice, spirit and movement of a character known as Mr. Bingle.

Bingle, a marionette snowman with an ice cream cone hat, wings of holly and a peppermint walking cane, is a character whose significance as part of New Orleans' popular cultural history should not be underrated. He emerged with television and the television generation, a playful salesman pitching Christmas toys sold at Maison Blanche department stores. Bingle was a star on local television back when there was only one station and when anything that moved on the tube was destined to become nostalgia.

But Bingle would transcend mere memories to become symbolic not only of the store, which hung a huge likeness of him on its facade each Christmas season, but of downtown. When Maison Blanche closed, Bingle's absence that following Christmas seemed to represent a troubled shopping district. Once Bingle returned to his perch the following Christmas, after new owners reopened the store, there seemed to be new hope for downtown.

There also seemed to be new fame for Bingle. When the MB chain was purchased by Goudchaux's department stores, part of the official announcement was that the purchase price had also included the rights to Bingle. The puppet had become corporate.

Though Bingle's stock had increased, much about him remained the same, notably the mannerisms and that distinguishable, one-and-only squeaky voice, the extension of Oscar Isentrout.

I first met Isentrout at what was a festive occasion, the opening night of the new Maison Blanche on Canal Street. The store was at its finest for inspection by the black-tie-and-evening-dress crowd. There was food, fashion, music, exhibits and, toward the back on the third floor, Isentrout and Mr. Bingle.

It was not a Bingle sort of crowd except for the few native-born baby boomers who happened to pass by, some of whom were too caught up in the sophistication of the evening to fully appreciate the moment. But Isentrout and his assistant persisted, re-introducing Bingle and staging the debut of a new character, Miss Blanche. Was there romance in Mr. Bingle's future?

Now, is there a future? Maison Blanche was quick to assure the public that the character would remain. But things change. His voice will be a little different from now on.

Isentrout was too busy to be interviewed that night — the show, after all, had to go on — other than to agree that we would get together someday. Since that day never came, I'm only left to draw conclusions from brief meetings Oscar Isentrout seemed to be a decent, simple man. He was the type most people in a crowded restaurant would not have even noticed. Yet for a generation of people in one little section of the world, he, more than anyone else, had the distinction of sounding like Christmas.

SPORTS

Opening Day

It was opening day of the 1985 major league baseball season and the lines outside the Superdome were long. During the winter the city had been granted an expansion franchise by the National League, so after years of waiting the New Orleans Pelicans were finally a big-league reality.

Some local fans there were at first had of mixed loyalties, since facing the Pels in their opening were none other than the Chicago Cubs. Without a team of its own, New Orleans had become a Cubs town, not only because of cable television which carries the team's games, but because New Orleanians identified easily with lovable losers. Even during the Cubs championship season the year before, New Orleanians felt a kinship with them. The heartbreak of the Cubs barely missing the World Series was no worse than that awful day a year earlier when a Rams field goal knocked the Saints out of the playoffs. New Orleanians knew defeat.

But on opening day Pelican fever was rampant, and no competing team could withstand it. The last bastion was the uptown Milan Bar where Cubs fans had gathered in past seasons for the telecasts. Now the bar's makeshift Wrigley Field bleachers had been removed in favor of Superdome seats. Gone were the Cubs pennants; this was Pelican country now.

On opening day the Superdome never looked better. Bunting was hung from different levels. The scoreboard had been overhauled and brought up to big league quality. Even the concessionaires, realizing that they must now serve major league hot dogs, plopped big juicy frankfurters on the grill, Chicago style.

Along the front row on the first base side, Governor Edwin Edwards and Mayor Morial met to toss out the first balls. Edwards used the occasion to quip that he always enjoyed "playing hardball with the mayor." To which Morial retorted, "Yeah, but sometimes you like to throw curves."

After the ceremony was over, there was thunder from the crowd of 60,000 as the New Orleans Pelicans took the field.

Pitching for the Pelicans that day was Vida Blue, a Louisiana native former superstar whose troubled career had been revived by the Pels. Rick Sutcliffe, the league's best pitcher from the previous season, was to be Blue's opposition. If Blue was in form, the game would be a pitcher's duel.

And in form he was. The eager crowd cheered Blue's pitches as Cub batters walked back to the dugout. The only performance as good as Blue's was Sutcliffe's, whose repertoire kept the Pelicans off base as well.

It was a duel until the top of the ninth inning, when Blue made his one mistake, a high pitch that crossed home plate a little too softly. Cubs catcher Jody Davis sent the season's first home run into the center field upper deck. The Pels came to bat in the last inning trailing by one run.

Sutcliffe was not anxious to do favors, striking out the first two batters. But then there was a break. The crowd came to life as Pelican shortstop Ken Oberkfell came to bat. Some of the fans remembered the little infielder from when he had played in New Orleans one season for a minor league team also called the Pelicans. They remembered his ability to draw a base on balls. His magic was still there. Sutcliffe tried but couldn't avoid throwing a ball four.

It was a classic baseball confrontation. Bottom of the ninth, two outs, the home team, losing by one but with a man on base. Sixty thousand New Orleanians felt numb. At the Milan Bar all orders were on hold.

By rights it was Vida Blue's turn to bat, but the fans knew better as they looked towards the dugout for a pinch hitter. There was a murmur, then applause and then a cheer as a figure walked out of the dugout. As the pinch hitter swung the warmup bats, those in the crowd noticed his muscular shoulders and the edge of slight reddish blond sideburn from beneath his helmet. The cheers were amplified as the announcement was made, "Batting for Vida Blue, Rusty Staub."

In recent times there has been only one bona fide New Orleanian to star in the majors and that is Staub. Some in the crowd could remember seeing him wearing a Jesuit High School uniform, leading the prep league in everything worthwhile; now they were seeing Staub in the dome with New Orleans written across his chest.

There was so much noise in the dome that even Edwards and Morial had to stop their private conversation. There are times when baseball matters more than politics.

Sutcliffe seemed affected by the cheers vibrating from the ceiling. Wrigley Field never sounded like that. He was so affected that his first three pitches were all high — three balls, and the crowd was in a frenzy.

But one does not become baseball's best without composure. He took hold of the situation and fired strike one. Taking the signal from catcher Davis, the Cub pitcher rocked back again and launched another pitch — Staub swung and missed. "Strike two."

This was the stuff of high sports drama. Bottom of the ninth, two outs, two strikes and three balls on the hometown hero. Sutcliffe and Staub eyed each other.

There was now silence, not only in the dome but at the Milan Bar, as Sutcliffe began the motions for his pitch. One hundred-twenty thousand eyes watched as a sphere was hurled ninety feet. Staub saw it coming, tightened his wrists and stepped into a swing. He met the ball with a mighty smash.

Somewhere in this land a brass band plays, and that evening it played in Chicago. The patrons at the Milan Bar sat there stunned as they watched the re-play of Cubs outfielder Gary Matthews who seemed to come from out of nowhere, made an impossible leap and caught the ball on the edge of homerun territory. "Holy cow!" Cubs announcer Harry Caray exclaimed.

But after the shock there would be joy among New Orleans fans, too. Their team had lost, but at least there was a team. It was opening day in the majors, and no longer would games have to be played only in the imagination.

Mid-Season

(Note: Last April, this column took a wishful look at opening day for the New Orleans Pelicans baseball team which, it imagined, was an expansion team in the National League. This week, a look at the team's performance as of mid-season.)

It was what seemed to be that most fatal of all innings for the Pelicans, the ninth. As the visiting Cincinnati Reds were batting, the Pelicans were guarding a 2-1 lead. The first two Reds had been easy outs, a grounder and a pop-up, but with the home team only one out from a victory, there was nervousness in the Dome at the sight of Pete Rose.

Rose was an attraction but the Pelicans, in their half-season of existence, had proven that they could draw a crowd just on the strength of their own appeal to a city that had wanted a team of its own. The team's record of 28 wins and 57 losses was the worst in baseball, but the local fans really didn't expect much from a first-year expansion team, so there was little pressure and more fun.

There was also a boomlet in the usually sluggish local summertime economy. A crowd of 63,000 packed the Dome for a July 4 header against the Dodgers. Delta Air Lines arranged a package weekend for fans from Atlanta when the Braves came to town. And Amtrak had to add extra cars to the Sunset Limited for Houstonians following the Astros to New Orleans. For years, the fan money had flowed in the opposite direction, New Orleans-to-Houston. Now it was coming back.

Part of the team's charm was its local touches- Louisianaians who had made it to the "bigs," like superstar Lou Brock, who had been talked out of retirement to coach third base. Then there was Vida Blue, who in his last outing had held the Cardinals for seven innings until they exploded. Two former UNO players, pitcher Eric Rasmussen and third baseman Augie Schmidt, were also on the roster but the crowd's favorite was clearly New Orleanaian Rusty Staub, who, rumor had it, was going to open a restaurant near the Dome.

For the old-timers at the Home Plate Inn on Tulane Avenue the team, by its existence, had shifted their conversation. No longer would they relive the memories of seasons long past; now the discussion was as current as yesterday's box score. At the Milan Lounge, the worship was no longer of some other city's team but of this city's own.

Sentiment, however, did not win ball games, as was apparent when Rose stopped at second base. He had turned a fast ball into a line drive to center field which hopped across the outfield fence. The umpire raised his arm, indicating a ground rule double.

Pelicans, real pelicans, were never as endangered as was the team's lead as right fielder Dave Parker approached the batter's box. Parker left no time for suspense as he stepped towards the first pitch, launching a missile which ricocheted off the right field wall. Meanwhile, Rose hustled as he never hustled before, miraculously seeming to round third in an instant. The ball was fielded and fired to the catcher. It was the tightest of matches, runner and sphere racing for home.

Only a few feet away from paydirt, Rose tried to outfly the ball as he dove for the plate. Both arrived at the same time — two blasts seeming to activate the umpire, whose arms shot up laterally as he yelled, "Safe!"

Lovable as they were, the Pels had blown another lead — or so it seemed.

Moments later, they were pouring beer over each other in the Pelican clubhouse while reliving the game's strange ending. After Rose's slide, catcher John Tamargo had thrown the ball to third baseman Schmidt, who had been frantically waving his arms. With the ball in hand, Schmidt touched third and pointed to the umpire, who shouted, "Out." In his hustle, in his desire to score faster than his legs could take him, Rose had not touched third base when turning for home.

It was not the prettiest way to win a ball game, but the Pelicans were hardly in a position to turn down ugly victories. Besides, it was the sort of win that they would be talking about at the Home Plate Inn 20 years from now. And it was an exciting way to begin the All-Star break.

At the Milan Bar, the three-day break seemed like too long a wait. There would be no Pelicans heading to the All-Star game, but if winning hearts were base hits the whole team would be heading to the Hall of Fame.

Post-Season

(Note: Last April this column first began charting the progress of the New Orleans Pelicans, an imaginary expansion team playing its first year of major league baseball. In July, the column looked at the team's progress as of the mid-season All Star break. This week, a final look at the team at season's end.)

Ozzie Smith of the Cardinals was at bat. The score was tied, 2-2, and the home team was hoping to win a game before going back on the road.

At the Home Plate Inn all eyes were on the television screen. They were eyes that had seen baseball a bit differently than in previous seasons because this year there had been a local big-league team to follow. But to no one's surprise, the rooting did not extend into the post-season playoffs because the Pelicans were left behind with the losers.

So the men in the Home Plate Inn, as well as the gang across town at the Milan Bar, were back to viewing other cities' teams as they watched Smith and the Cardinals tangle with the Dodgers.

There would be no pennant hanging in the Superdome this year — far from it. The expansion Pelicans had shown a little promise in April but by August and September, when the competition was familiar enough with the Pelican players to know how to beat them, losses were as frequent as afternoon showers.

It was not a glorious finish. The team had the worst batting average and the most generous pitching staff in the league. A survey in USA Today newspaper had asked National League players which town they enjoyed the most. New Orleans was the top selection, first for the food and second for the victories. It was a town of hot spice and easy wins.

Not much good could be said about the team, other than that none of its players were named in drug scandals and when the players' union's strike was over, all of the Pelicans returned to the team.

They returned, however, not so much because they had to but because, despite it all, there was a good spirit on the team. The newness and freshness of the team compensated for the losses. New Orleans, after all, is a city that has been waiting for nearly 20 years for the Saints to field a winner so not much can be demanded yet of the first-year Pelicans. Rookie errors can be viewed not so much as mistakes but as practical lessons for the future. There are no high expectations for the team other than to just become a part of the city. And that, the team did well this season. Pelican players were the rage, selling, in commercials, beer, fried chicken, used cars and even funeral plots. They were the heroes of fundraisers and shopping centers.

As a team, the Pelicans helped fill hotel rooms and, most of all, they filled the dome, not for every game, but often enough to prove that the city has embraced the team. Some Pelican players who would have been sent to the minors in other organizations were hitless wonders in New Orleans. They were dazed at the stardom that their .200 batting average had brought them.

Everything, of course, has its season and so does baseball. Some of the players were surprised when they returned from a road trip in August. They walked onto the dome's turf and noticed the pale outline of a football field. Those who love the game wince at the sight of a pitcher's mound intersected by a yardline stripe. Football, pinch hitter Rusty Staub explained to some of the younger players, is still king in this town — at least until the Pelicans become winners.

But within that kingdom, there are fiefdoms where baseball reigns supreme. As Ozzie Smith waited for his pitch, Staub and some of the Pelican players walked into the Milan Bar. They didn't need an introduction nor had they needed one earlier that day when the players visited the Home Plate Inn.

To the guys at the Milan the visit seemed to be a reward for their years of waiting for a team and the frustration of the first season. The beer flowed as fans and players sat around testing rumors that Staub would be the team's next manager and exchanging stories about the season. They were so immersed in each other that no one noticed Smith running around the bases with his arms in the air, celebrating his game-winning home run. Down in New Orleans, other cities' teams didn't matter as much because now the fans had their own stories to tell.

Pinstripes

That sound might have been forgotten, but I could suddenly hear it again, not actually, but in my mind — the scraping sound of metal spikes brushing against concrete. At the time it could have been the pounding of gladiator boots as their wearers entered the coliseum.

I was at a family picnic at City Park stadium and managed to stray away long enough to discover the ghosts of seasons past. Standing in the runway that opened to the playing field, the distant summer of '59 seemed vivid. That was the last year of the original New Orleans Pelicans, a minor league team that had lost its ballpark and was sentenced to spend its final two seasons playing in a football stadium. Each game night I followed the Pelicans along that path, a wide-eyed tagalong carrying bat bags and first aid kits, the tools of my spot in the starting lineup in the position of batboy.

From my perspective, down below, looking up, the Pelicans seemed magnificent in their hand-me-down Yankee pinstripe uniforms. Once a farm club of the big boys from the Bronx, the Pelicans in their last year were independents, baseball castoffs with uniforms to match. But that didn't matter along the runway, before the first pitch, when the evening's game was still winnable and heroics were still possible. Along the railings kids dangled programs with hopes for an autograph.

Standing there last week, remembering it all, I thought back to first baseman Hal "Tookie" Gilbert, a New Orleans native who had made it to the majors and was then on the way down, spending his last days on the baseball diamond as a favorite son. Those men walking onto the field were a magnificent sight, from the back looking not much different from Mantle or Maris or even Gehrig or DiMaggio.

On the field, however, the perfomance was noticably different. The Pelicans, playing in the Southern Association, finished seventh out of eight teams. The hitting was mediocre and the pitching was bad. The team did lead the league in one admirable category, however. One evening my back was turned from the field while I talked to the trainer when there was a sudden roar from the stands. That in itself was startling because there was usually little to cheer about. As the Pelican infield trotted off the field its members were congratulating each other. "That is the Pelicans' second triple play of the season," the field announcer stated. "They now lead the league in that category." I had seen every home game but missed the big play. Would that be a metaphor of life?

In retrospect, the more accurate metaphor was the Pelicans leaving the field, despite their best efforts. There would be no next season. The team moved to Little Rock, the league headquarters left the city. New Orleans, the largest city in the Association, seemed shamed. If only the city had a proper ballpark, the arguments began, then maybe it could support its own teams.

But there would always be those who could appreciate something even in the simplest of settings. The Pelicans were a scruffy, sometimes profane, lot playing in a makeshift ballpark but nevertheless off on the most basic of American adventures — pursuing a championship. There was no magic to the way it all ended but to those who cared the magic came from sharing the dream while it lasted.

Moose

It cost $8.50 for a box seat at the New York Yankees-Montreal Expos pre-season game in the Superdome, but I would have been willing to throw in a few extra if I had known Moose was going to be sitting behind me.

That wasn't my first impression, though, as I found my way to my seat. "Hi, I'm Moose," this burly character said, extending his hand. It seemed like he might be just another drunk showing off, but then I didn't know Moose yet. It turned out that by the time I arrived, Moose had pretty much made the acquaintance of all those around him. He was not going to spend the next nine innings of his life all alone.

"What kind of barbecue sauce does your momma use?" he asked, for no apparent reason, the boy sitting next to him. "Is it Kraft? Open Pit? Blue Plate? You just haven't lived until you've had barbecue with Open Pit sauce."

Rat-ta-tat-ta-tat. . . Suddenly someone about 20 rows up was blowing a botched version of "charge" on a trumpet. Heads turned towards the trumpeteer, and Moose began to laugh. "Hey, that's Ralph! Play that trumpet, Ralph!" Moose turned back, looked towards the field and spotted someone on the first row. "Hey Frank! Look, that's Ralph playing the trumpet."

A lifetime of introducing himself to practically everone in sight had evolved inevitably into his knowing a lot of people, even some that one wouldn't ordinarily have expected. "Hey, Winfield, remember me?" Moose shouted as the slugging star of the New York Yankees walked towards home plate. "You and I used to play ball together. The only difference is that now you make a million dollars!"

Dave Winfield was too far away to hear the yell, but Moose's memories weren't distant at all. He told those of us around him about an amateur tournament he once played in Nebraska, when Winfield was on an opposing team.

Moose had apparently had his day, when he was a svelte young man and dreams were cheap. He played ball well enough to win a high school scholarship and then, like all good ballplayers, he hoped for something bigger. "How did you do in the tournament?" someone asked Moose. "I hit one ball 360 feet," Moose answered, "only, the fence was 365 feet away."

Only a baseball game allows characters like Moose to develop. Football and basketball are too frantic, with the constant standing, yelling, jumping up and down. But baseball, with its slower pace, provides time for conversation and camaraderie. "I can't believe I'm sitting here getting drunk watching a baseball game," Moose muttered, then smiled, "I could be sitting home getting drunk watching 'Love Boat'."

Moose's era was the 1960's, his high school days when he was a big man on the ball diamond. He was the kind of guy who hung around with all the athletes and who knew all the rock band musicians and their dates. "Tell me where you went to high school," he asked people around him. "Did you know. . . " The high school stars of his day stood out in his mind like old Sam Cooke records. His memories swirled at 45 rpm.

"What time is it?" Moose asked rhetorically while squinting at the scoreboard's digital clock. "I could be home watching 'Fantasy Island.' Right now Tattoo would be saying, de plane, de plane.'"

In the bottom of the eighth, the Yankees had a rally going, so Moose took charge of the situation. "Hey Ralph, play that charge," Moose hollered. Ralph did and the Yankees scored. "Can you believe I once played ball with Dave Winfield?" he asked.

In the top of the ninth the Expos failed to score, thus falling in defeat to the Yankees. It was time to leave. "Hey kid," Moose commanded the boy next to him, "if your momma ever fixes some crayfish etouffee invite me over."

I filed past Moose who at the moment was acting like a father of the bride, receiving congratulations from the passing crowd. "Well, Moose," I said, "it was an honor meeting you."

"Maybe we'll see each other next year," he answered. "What's your name again?"

For the record, in the seventh inning Dave Winfield hit a home run that fell several rows beyond the left field wall. But that night, in that ballpark, in the presence of the mighty New York Yankees, it was Moose who was the star of the game.

Bum

"This one right here," Bum Phillips said, pointing to his pickup truck parked in the lot at the Saints' David Drive camp. Moments later, we were heading along Veterans Boulevard with Bum steering. He had just arrived in New Orleans and was having trouble finding a place to graze horses, but that didn't matter; his main concern was to make the Saints a winning team. He would be busy.

Our interview was conducted over lunch at Augie's, where I quickly learned something from Phillips about New Orleans food. "The steaks!" the coach exclaimed with his classic drawl. "The worst steak I've had in New Orleans is better than the best steak I ever had in Texas." Bum, it seemed, was going to like it here.

It was hard to ignore the reaction from the other customers in the restaurant. As kids, they had seen cowboys chasing Indians on television. As adults, they had seen this cowboy too on TV, only he was standing on the sidelines, in pursuit of not only Redskins, but Bears, Lions, and even Steelers. As he entered the restaurant, Phillips had flipped his Stetson on top of a pantry. Any polite cowboy knows not to wear his hat when he comes in from off the range. Polite cowboys also know not to turn away customers who ask for autographs. There were many interruptions during the interview.

Phillips spoke with that folksy, anecdotal style that made him so quotable. "I can take criticism," he explained. "Once in Houston my mother came to see a game. It was the first game she ever saw me coach. After the game she said, 'Y'all weren't very good, son.' She was right — we stunk that day."

As for the Saints, why had the team that he had just taken command of performed so poorly the season before? "The same ole problem," Phillips answered. "Too many chiefs and not enough Indians." How many chiefs would there be on the team this season? He held up a forefinger — one. This cowboy was going to be the boss Indian.

As it happens, even chiefs must answer to a higher authority. I thought of that lunch with Phillips after he resigned under pressure from the Saints last week. A few days after that interview, I had received a note from him thanking me for joining him at lunch.

I should have been the one to send a letter instead.

These days, they're trying to analyze just what happened to Phillips' regime as coach. Some are saying that his style was too old-fashioned. Such an approach may not do much for winning football games but it is a trait that makes for classy departures. In an era when sports contracts are violated routinely, Phillips asked that his be voided. He wouldn't wait around to be dismissed and then collect money for not working. That's not the way of the range. I recalled something he said in that interview five years earlier. When asked how long it would take to make the team a winner, Phillips responded that if he couldn't do it in five years he should be fired. Bum saw his own prophecy and faced it with dignity.

One day soon, a new Saints coach will be called to speak for the Saints' future. Somewhere in that conversation there should be some mention about the occasional loose talk which suggests that victories are not as important as how the game is played. If only that were true, then Bum Phillips could have retired knowing that he had won the big one.

Cheers

Even people of whom you would never expect it are asking the question. I'm talking about reserved, dignified people, who know so little about football that they think Bum Phillips is a defective screwdriver. These people are reciting the chant. They're discussing it on the radio and on the front page of the Times-Picayune. The chant is all over town: "Who dat? Who dat? Who dat say dey gonna beat dem Saints?"

As a bit of New Orleans lexicon the chant will be a classic. It is seemingly ethnic in origin but spans ethnicity, being spoken by folks of all races and classes. But, could the phrase be modified to include even more people? Granted, much of the rhythm is lost in changing the wording, but perhaps different groups could relate to the cheer better if it were put in their tongue. Bureaucrats and memo writers, for example, could march along while singing in unison:

"Who was the person (male and/or female) whose input football-wise questioned whether speculation of a victory by the Saints was a viable alternative?"

Then there are news people, the kind who live by the style book, who might enliven the pressroom by chanting:

"Which person made the alleged remark, according to reliable sources, about the possible defeat of the New Orleans Saints football team?"

Since there are some grammatical flaws in the original "Who Dat" cheer, language purists, English professors and snobs may prefer to rally behind the team with a rousing cry:

"By whom was the question raised whether or not the Saints would win?"

Maybe modification is the wrong approach. "Who Dat" belongs by itself without imitations. Even if Antoine's tried to fix Popeye's chicken, it wouldn't seem the same. Some things must maintain their own peculiarities, and that goes for cheers, too. A better idea may be to develop entirely new chants targeted at specific groups. There could be an Uptowners' cheer:

Go Saints Go, win the chalice
Then we'll meet at Commander's Palace.

And of course, no one could overlook the good ole everyday New Orleans Yat, who would join his buddies in hollering:

Crawfish, crabs, Dixie Beer
Come on Saints. kick'em in the rear.

As is being proven with the "Who Dat" cheer, these ditties can even get national publicity. So, we can take advantage of the promotional value by nicknaming the Saints' defense in honor of the World's Fair's main attraction:

Come on Saints, make 'em fall
When they hit the Wonder Wall.

A City Hall cheer could further encourage the defense by urging that they contain the opposing offensive units:

Rah, rah Saints, jail those worms
Make 'em serve unlimited terms.

There's no guarantee that any of these cheers will help the Saints win more football games, but at the very least they should make people wonder, "Who dat sayin' all dem cheers?"

Say It Ain't So, John

TO: *John Mecom, Owner*
New Orleans Saints

Dear John:

I'm reminded these days of the story from the baseball scandals of 1919 when Shoeless Joe Jackson of the Chicago White Sox was called to court to answer to charges that he accepted money from gamblers for affecting the outcome of games. As he entered the court building, a waif of a newspaper boy spotted his hero and hollered in disbelief those now immortal words, "Say it ain't so, Joe!" As stories continue about the Saints possibly being sold and perhaps moving to Jacksonville, I, with equal disbelief, find myself wanting to echo those sentiments — say it ain't so, John! Don't hurt this city.

John, there are few institutions that have had an emotional hold on New Orleans as have the Saints. That emotion began even long before you became involved with the franchise. There were years when New Orleans, then a fading has-been city, was trying to regain respectability. In modern America, a professional sports franchise had become a symbol of progress and New Orleans wanted to be progressive. For several years, civic-minded promoters lured NFL teams to stage exhibition games in our town so that we could prove our worthiness and willingness to support pro football. To sweeten the deal we talked about building the biggest and best stadium of all, and politicians and businessmen formed committees and waged campaigns to see it built.

This town even changed its social attitudes for pro football. When the All Star game for the old American Football League, which was to be played here, was cancelled because black players refused to play in a segregated town, the citizens berated themselves. Local laws, and some attitudes, were changed to make the city officially integrated. This town wanted badly to be professional.

Finally that grand day came when the commissioner announced that New Orleans would receive an NFL franchise — and oh, by the way, he hinted, wouldn't it be nice if the voters of the state approved an amendment allowing the construction of a domed stadium. Euphoria carried the day, and the election as well; the city got the team and its stadium, too.

That pride overflowed during the Saints' very first game, when John Gilliam ran back the opening kickoff for a touchdown. This town was crazy — imagine a team that had only been playing football for thirty seconds but was already leading the Rams 7-0. There was talk of a dynasty.

Since then, we've heard more about disappointment than dynasty but the city has still supported its team — even after the bad seasons, even after 16 years of never having a winner. New Orleans is a forgiving lover, although frequently hurt if it remains supportive. Who dat saying this town ain't loyal?

I don't think that any sports team can ever mean as much to this city as has the Saints' franchise. It was our first major league team, the expansion franchise we have nurtured since birth. In the world of big-time sports, both you and the city have grown up and matured together.

In fact, even if the Saints never play another down in New Orleans, you are already a part of the city's history. I had hoped your tenure would be a happy one rather than one that ends with a bitter parting. Losing seasons can easily be forgotten when there are memories of a championship trophy and a victory parade down Canal Street. Sell the team if you must, but keep it in New Orleans, where you will always be remembered as a part of the team this city fought to have.

Ironically, this talk about the city losing the Saints comes in the year that was supposed to be good one for New Orleans — with the Sun King, the Vatican Treasures, the new exhibition hall, the fair, new hotels — this town, like the Saints after that 1-15 season, was going to make a comeback. That's why I implore you to say it ain't so, John, because the city has tried hard to improve itself. Losing the Saints would be a major blow to the city's morale. Dammit, New Orleans deserves better than that.

The Forgotten League

I happened to hear a score from the playoffs in the National Basketball Association. The score itself did not mean anything to me, but it served as a reminder that another season has passed in which I did not watch on television nor pay attention at all to the results of any NBA games. The protest continues.

There are bitter feelings about the NBA in New Orleans, and mine are among them. The league once had a successful franchise in this city, one that still holds several NBA attendance records, but then the ownership fell into the wrong hands and the New Orleans Jazz was moved to Salt Lake City. The owner didn't even have the decency to change the team's nickname, a name that reflected its birthplace. To call a team the "Utah Jazz" is about as incongruous as the "New Orleans Tabernacle Choir." So the sobriquet "Jazz" remains behind some other place's name — a box score reminder of a city that was snubbed.

This sort of unjust franchise shifting is becoming more commonplace nowadays. People in Oakland and Baltimore no doubt feel the same pain over the loss of the Raiders and the Colts that New Orleanians have felt over the Jazz. But there was a legal difference in the Jazz situation that made the parent league look distinctly gutless. The Jazz shift happened before the Oakland Raiders case, the case in which courts ultimately ruled, in effect, that leagues could not stop franchises from relocating. At the time of the Jazz move the precedent was in favor of the leagues — they still had the authority to prevent owners from moving their teams. Both baseball and football had begun to stand firm against such moves.

But not the NBA. One owner was quoted conceding that New Orleans deserved to keep the team but that he would vote to allow the switch because he might need the favor returned some day. Lawrence O'Brien, the commissioner, whom I had once admired, stood by quietly like a referee afraid to blow the whistle. If Pete Rozelle had been NBA commissioner then, the Jazz would probably still be here. Instead, a financially troubled league refused to make the call against one of its owners. There were meetings and pleas for both sides to work out their differences, but never a firm position.

When basketball season began again, New Orleans was left only with tattered bumper stickers from the team it supported, and memories, such as that evening during the team's first season when, after having lost its first 20 games, the Jazz rallied in the final seconds and Pete Maravich hit the winning shot at the buzzer. Since the Superdome wasn't complete yet, the team played its early home games at either the

Municipal Auditorium or Loyola's Field House. On Good Friday that year, the Jazz played the Knicks and packed the auditorium. It was a happy crowd. The team won a squeaker.

Maravich would have his big nights in the dome too, such as the game when he accounted for 69 points. The crowd was in a frenzy — partially for Maravich, partially because the Jazz were going to win and partially because Burger King gave free French fries, in exchange for a ticket stub, every time the Jazz scored 110 points or more. Even though the team generally finished near last place in the standings, Burger King still had to frequently make good its fries offer. There were also the side shows. During half-time fans could try to make a goal from half-court. If they connected, and I recall that only one or two ever did, they won a new car. Hot Rod Hundley, the team's radio announcer, coined an often-repeated phrase in reference to the times when guard Aaron James made a long goal. Mimics around town repeated Hot Rod's excited description — "A.J. from the parking lot!"

There was also the last game of the 1978 season — Fan Appreciation Night. During half-time, prizes were given to spectators whose faces were captured by the dome's television camera and shown on the big screen. None of us fans who were being appreciated that night knew that was to be the last New Orleans Jazz game. For me it was my last NBA game as well.

Last season, however, I did discover that my resentment is probably reversible. When promoter Barry Mendelson was actively trying to bring Cleveland's NBA team (which at the time was for sale) to New Orleans, I found myself excited by the possibility. The NBA really hurt this town by abandoning it, but that doesn't mean that we couldn't welcome it back. Bringing to town some regular season games by other cities' teams is fine but it's not the same as getting back our own team. Until that happens, I'll remember the league as the one in which the owners, more than the players, commit the fouls.

LOCAL BRANDS

Have A Dixie

It is time for us New Orleanians to get serious about Dixie Beer.

Times are tough for the little brewery and as this is written there's reason to believe its future may be in jeopardy. If it goes under, the city will lose not only jobs but an important tax source. It will also lose a bit of pride. We see it happen over and over, businesses that tried to hang on but couldn't. Have you noticed that you don't see as many New Orleanians drinking Big Shot Cola any more?

Dixie isn't selling well lately, not even in New Orleans. What's frustrating is that there is no good reason why it doesn't outsell its competitors. Beer is a hocus-pocus sort of industry. People select their brands largely in response to an image created by advertising. The national competitors have the resources to project soothing associations between their beer and the country of 1100 springs or cool mountain water or he-men celebrating after-hours in a bar. In the face of such heavy advertising, it's hard for a small brewery to compete.

There would be no point in suggesting that locals should buy Dixies for the sake of local pride if the product were inferior to others, but it's not. The one fact that brewers know but that beer drinkers deny is that all beers are basically the same, and, yes, beers of a kind taste alike. Beer drinkers will argue vocally that they can tell their Budweiser and Miller from their Dixie, but it's a claim that seldom holds up under taste tests. If you don't believe it, try for yourself. Buy several different brands of beers, conceal their identity, then have the gang list which beer is which. See how quickly the boasting is contradicted.

But even those who insist that they can detect the fine difference could most likely only do so in a true beer-tasting situation. Like wine, beer has to be carefully tasted, fully utilizing the taste buds in a controlled situation. But when the suds are used to wash down boiled crayfish or an oyster po-boy those subtle differences are overpowered — beer is beer.

What's ironic about the situation is that New Orleanians like to think of themselves as a unique people, with their own quirks and tastes. Yet in the face of mass marketing, we're just as vulnerable as anyone else — network programming draws larger audiences than local shows, McDonald's and Wendy's are popular and Bud and Miller outsell Dixie.

What is needed is for Dixie to become a local cause. At a time when several new beers have come into the local market we have to stick with Dixie, if for no other reason than that it is in our best interest to do so. Sure, the national beers give jobs to local distributors, but that's like selling Toyotas in Detroit. We need not only the distribution but the manufacturing, too. Dixie has to become New Orleans' Chrysler.

I, too, have had my flirtations with the national beers. After work, I sometimes wonder if it is indeed Miller time; and if Budweiser is the king of beers it can't be bad — and besides, I like the Clydesdales. I also have a sentimental attachment for Pabst ever since I visited its brewery in Milwaukee and ended the tour awash in free samples. But I'll be buying Dixie from now on.

I'll do so because it's a good beer and it's good for the city. Its presence provides an anchor for Tulane Avenue, a dying street trying to make a comeback. It's also good for local pride. I'll be buying Dixie because if I and others don't, then perhaps sooner than we think, every night, as the jingle says, may begin to look like a Stroh's Light night.

New Orleans can't afford to let too many good things get away.

Hello Mello Jax

A cowboy and his horse each took a seat on a stool in a barroom. "Bartender," the cowboy said, "I'd like a glass of Jax for me and my horse Elwood."

Well, as might be expected the bartender was indignant. "I'm sorry," he shouted, "we just do not serve beer to dumb animals, see that sign over there (which read: NO BEER SERVED TO HORSES). If we serve one horse we'll have to serve them all."

Sadly the cowboy turned to his steed and spoke, "I'm sorry Elwood." The sad-eyed trotter glanced back, shrugged his shoulders and responded, "That's okay, I'm driving anyway."

Memories are a bit fuzzy now but the new development at the old Jax brewery has triggered recollections of the days when Jax was a thriving business. Curiously, to the children of the '60s the brewery will be remembered not so much for its suds as for its commercials. Jax was a major local advertiser and, in retrospect, a major part of the story of early television in the city.

Back in the days when advertisers purchased entire programs, Jax sponsored the sports news on WDSU, at the time the only television station in town. Each weekday evening young Mel Leavitt would deliver the scores on the Jax World of Sports. During the commercial breaks a chorus would sing what in fact may have been the best known song in town, "Hello mello Jax little darlin', you're the beer for me, yessiree."

As the television market became more competitive the brewery needed to find a gimmick, and did just that with a series of commercial cartoons. The then little known husband and wife team of Mike Nichols and Elaine May wrote the scripts which became a prime subject of schoolyard conversation. "Hey, didja see the one about the cowboy who took his horse to a bar and the bartender said. . ."

Another cartoon featured a man who boasted that his dog could talk. Challenged to prove his claim, the man posed a question to his hound, "What's on top of a house?" "Ruffff" the dog barked. "And when I'm playing golf too hard, and I hit the ball too hard, where does it go?" Again the dog responded, "Rufff." A skeptical bystander then decided to pose his own question: "Who was the only U.S. President to be elected to three consecutive terms?" The dog and his master both looked confused. Obviously perplexed the dog stammered for an answer: "Rrr. . . rrr. . . Coolidge?"

Then there was the articulate cartoon character who criticized a colleague for not being able to properly deliver the line, "Drink Jax, it's the real beer." The articulate one ended the segment by announcing to the audience, "Drink Rax, it's the beal jeer."

Those commercials made TV viewers laugh, although the boys in the Jax board room would have no doubt had a few chuckles themselves if the public outside was guffawing less and drinking more. Still Jax would continue to keep us entertained.

For example, a new commercial campaign introduced a character named Andrew Fabacher who bore a striking resemblance both in apperarance and in dress to Andy Jackson himself. In an apparent attempt to capitalize on and to popularize the name of the Fabacher family which ran the brewery, some ad agent concocted a story whereby General Andy Fabacher was miffed that the beer was called Jax (after Jackson) and not Fabacher. History apparently had confused its characters and Andrew Fabacher was the city's real hero. "Drink Fabacher Beer," the general would announce while displaying a bottle of Jax.

It's not known whether or not that campaign increased the fortunes of anyone other than the actor who got to make public apperarances around town while mounted on his charger leading his campaign to right history's inaccuracies. Once again Jax entertained.

In the end, Jax would be beaten at its own game. As creative and ambitious as its advertising campaigns were, no regional brewery could compete with big budget beers that made Milwaukee famous.

As the British must have realized when they were trounced by Andy Fabacher's armies at Chalmette, no matter how fancy your red coat is, sometimes you just can't reverse the course of events.

Gold Seal And Others

I confess that before last week I never gave Gold Seal Creameries more than ten minutes' thought in my life. But suddenly, since its announced closing, it seems like it will be hard to live without it. There have been stories, many stories, about New Orleans families raised on nothing but Gold Seal products. "They had the best quality milk in town," someone said, "and their ice cream was really underrated."

We're hearing now about the dairy's ricotta cheese, which was specially made to stuff the perfect cannoli. Italian restaurants are worried about a suitable replacement cheese for their lasagna. The chocolate milk was the best there was, I'm told. And Creole cream cheese will never be the same.

What happened to Gold Seal is an old story that this city has witnessed so many times before. There will be tales of a soft economy and changing consumer habits, but the main reason why there is only one brewery left is the same as why the local recording industry failed — national competition. The networks and the highways have killed off regional manauafacturers because the national brands have the dollars for advertising and the resources to get shelf space. Gold Seal was left to the mom and pop stores in an era when mom and pop were getting tired. The dairy's milk may have been superior, but quality is not a sacred cow.

I wish we had a second chance at using Gold Seal products, but it's too late. That's what hurts. There is something wrong about businesses being appreciated only in the past tense. The Gold Seal experience has made me want to take roll call on other regional manafacturers who feel the same heat from national competion but have somehow perserved. We may not appreciate them quite enough.

There is, of course, Dixie Beer, defying the odds by staying alive. It now uses spring water but Budweiser still outsells it in its own hometown.

We may be an unparalleled capitol for homemade root beers, either Barq's or Big Shot. Few cities can claim two regional soft drink manufacturers.

A cold Barq's is all the better for washing down a po-boy which is made all the better by Blue Plate mayonnaise. No national brand makes a better mayonnaise. That's something to relish.

On the 500 block of First Street, the Turnbull Cone Company makes not only ice cream cones but Melba toast, all the better for spreading on some of Baumer Foods' Crystal preserves.

A character named Savory Simon still decorates the packages of Hubig's fried pies.

And, Zatarain's and Rex are both the regional and national names for crab boils.

This is not a complete list, but it will never be very long. Too many companies have already gone the way of either Regal Beer, a name remembered just on memorabilia, or Jax, a label sold off tho another company. The economy and the times have been tough. But while the second chance with Gold Seal is denied, it isn't with the other places. It is better, after all, to appreciate things before, rather than after, they're gone.

Mrs. Drake

When I was in grade school, lunch came with a label on it. The school didn't have a cafeteria so we ordered sandwiches from Mrs. Drake, the local supplier of pre-made sandwiches-to-go tagged with a label assuring us that the contents were "fresh daily." To the side of the label was a sketch of a smiling duck wearing a chef's hat and an apron — Mrs. Drake, we presumed.

Through eighth grade we got to know the sandwich choices quite well, choices which included luncheon meat and pickle, tuna, roast beef and the daring luncheon meat and potato salad. There was occasional variation, such as the time Mrs. Drake excited the student body by introducing the Little Barbecue, a sandwich which not only had the appeal of barbecue flavoring but that came on a bun. rather than the usual sliced white bread. Everyone who was anyone in the school's fashionable set was dining on a Little Barbecue.

Since grade school, Mrs. Drake and I have fallen apart. Thoughts of her, through the years, were mostly nostalgic whenever I saw reminders, such as when passing her headquarters on Canal Street near Broad, or seeing one of her sandwiches, waiting to be sold, on a convenience store counter. Like Nehis and popsicles, Mrs. Drake just seemed to belong to the past.

But then I found myself working in the Maison Blanche building where there is a snack shop on the first floor with fare that includes Mrs. Drake sandwiches. I write with a word processor now instead of a number two lead pencil, but once again I find myself sitting at a desk during lunch, eating a Mrs. Drake sandwich.

In this rediscovery phase, what is most surprising is how little the sandwiches have changed. They cost more, obviously, and the wrapping is a bit different, but the label, the one with the yellow duck, is still the same. Most of all, the sandwiches still taste exactly as they did back back in grade school — neither time nor competition has altered the preparation.

To me, the luncheon meat and pickle is the quintessential Mrs. Drake sandwich. It is simple — two slices of luncheon meat. a dash of mayonnaise and mustard and a pickle — but the combination works as though there is a time sequence for the flavors, with the pickle programmed to add the kick at the end. In the age of the soybean, no one messed with Mrs. Drake's recipes.

Since this rediscovery, it has occurred to me that Mrs. Drake's sandwiches may be the most underrated food in New Orleans, if for no other reason than survivability. The company has withstood the onslaught of fast food places and sales have remained steady while grand restaurants have folded.

In fact, probably no local food business in the city's history has provided more workday lunches than Mrs. Drake. From the energy that comes from the combination of a Mrs. Drake, a Barq's root beer and a Hubig's pie, streets have been paved, bridges built, contracts signed and columns written.

Columns that end with the satisfaction of speculating that somewhere in this city someone is having a Mrs. Drake's sandwich and a New Coke and realizing that the taste of some things should never change.

FOOD

Bun On The Run

Down the block I could see the sign for Galatoire's as I, too, prepared for Vieux Carre dining. "Give me one, small, without onions," I told the chef, who quickly complied.

With an artist's precision he dipped his tongs into the vat within his Lucky Dog cart and pulled out the steaming sausage. Just as the great chefs build a crust around their beef Wellington, this vendor placed the wiener into a bun and, for his sauce, used a squirt of mustard, followed by a dash of chili.

"We use Frey wieners," he explained, with the pride of a restaurant boasting of his prime filets, "they're 100 percent beef."

Without any prodding he continued: "These are pretty good hot dogs. A lot of local people eat them too. We use our own special chili. I've had some people come here and say these are better than the hot dogs at Coney Island."

His was a well-organized kitchen. Within moments my meal was served, but that created an unanticipated problem. Where does one eat a Lucky Dog? The dog comes wrapped only in a napkin, hardly enough to keep it warm until you get home. The other possibility is to eat it right there on the spot, but that creates the risk of someone you know seeing you — standing there on Bourbon Street — eating a Lucky Dog.

I stayed anyway, naturally, because it was a cold evening and there were few people on the street. Also, because the chef had quite a tale.

"I came down here from Boston a few months ago to get away from the cold," he explained, while shivering and laughing to himself. He was quite articulate and his voice was deep and resonant. "Well, I got here with $1,000, but then on New Year's Eve night I was jacked and lost $500. Can you believe that, they took $500."

At that, the conversation was interrupted to allow time for some marketing. When he had opened the vat to fish out my hot dog he had been impressed by the cloud of steam. He reasoned that if he would open the vat again the aroma within would help lure customers to his cart. Moments later, the air was filled with the essence of weenies.

How does he enjoy the work?

"It's all right," he answered, "you get to meet a lot of people."

Will he stay in town through Mardi Gras?

"I think so," he replied. "Some of the old-timers tell me that during carnival we can make $150 to $200 a day."

And the World's Fair?

"May as well stay around for that, too."

By this time I had finished the Lucky Dog, an accomplishment which qualified me to offer the following critique. To the negative, the Lucky Dog suffers from the wieners being boiled. Any hot dog, regardless of the quality of the meat, should be either grilled, roasted, or broiled. Boiling deadens the flavor. Also, it would help if the buns could be warmed, something that shouldn't be too difficult considering the steam coming from the cart.

But still, it's not a bad hot dog. It is as good as most commercial hot dogs, and even better that the small hot dog (but not the Super dog) at the Superdome. It's a decent product that has somehow gotten a bum rap through the years. The Lucky Dog deserves more respect.

Meanwhile, another customer had arrived — a portly gentleman, apparently a visiting gourmet, dressed in gray pants, a gray jacket, wearing a gray helmet and riding a gray motorcycle, who pulled up alongside the cart, thereby taking advantage of its roadside service capacity.

Knowing that I was occupying space that could be taken by another customer, I left. My route took me past Galatoire's, where I felt that those inside who were feasting on the canape Lorenzo and the chicken Clemenceau had nothing over me — for on that evening, I had experienced the chien chaud.

Muffuletta Row

By my count there were 13 different brands of olive oil stacked on the shelves at the Central Grocery, the city's senior, and one of the few remaining, truly neighborhood Italian grocery stores. Most of the brands claimed to contain virgin olive oil although there seemed to be differences in degree, with some claiming that their oil was extra virgin. And that was just the olive oil in cans; stacked in other spots throughtout the store were bottles of the stuff, at least four brands before I stopped counting.

Olives are essential to the business at the Decatur Street grocery, not only by the can but in its main product — the one which the store made famous and in turn for which the store has become famous — the definitive New Orleans muffuletta.

There are counters for eating in the grocery, an accommodation for those who choose to chew while taking in the ambiance of the grocery, which has been operated by the Tusa family since 1905. The menu is simple — muffulettas, which can be purchased whole ($4) or half ($2.50), or something described as the "original deluxe" version which costs $4.85 and comes stacked with extra meat.

Not that the regular muffulettas aren't filling. Sandwiched into the soft slices of Italian bread are layers of salami, ham and cheese covered with another layer of olive salad. It is the latter that is the most important, for what sauce is to spaghetti, olive salad is to the muffuletta. Central's salad is a magnificent concoction with not only slivers of green olive but bits of marinated vegetables, including cauliflower. The olive oil oozes into the top slice of the bread, keeping it moist but not drippy.

There is no setting quite as appropriate for devouring a muffuletta. The place must not look too different from the days when local Sicilians shopped there, not only when trying to recreate native dishes, but because it was the neighborhood grocery. The old ceiling fans still distribute the aroma of coffee beans and spices throughout the store. A whole dried cod sits in a box on the counter; dried beans, including the red, are available from sacks. Pasta is provided in seemingly more forms than there are brands of olive oil. Practically every other item seems to be flavored with either anise or almond. The Central could just as easily satisfy the needs of a kitchen in Palermo.

"If he wants a sample, let him go to Goldberg's and get a sample." So kidded one of the workers in response to a customer's request. Goldberg's is the men's clothing store next door, a place that seems to belong as much to another era as does the Central. In fact the entire 900 block of Decatur Street across from the French Market still seems to be in the

1930s. It is a block of small businesses, most stereotypical — a Jewish clothing store, an Italian grocery, and sandwich shops. It is a block that has remained genuine.

The block could be called Muffuletta Row because the Central is not alone in dispensing the sandwich. To one side is the Progress grocery where the sign claims that the family of B. Perrone & Sons is now in its third generation of business, which includes serving muffulettas. To the other side is Frank's sandwich shop, where another sign announces that the three generations of Gaglianos have been slicing Genoa salami. On the other blocks things have changed with times and taste, but muffuletta Row is one of those places that has survived time by remaining the same.

Crawfish Eating

It's time that the truth be told. Here we are in the state that provides 99 percent of the crawfish eaten throughout the world, yet — and this is the shocking part — there are people living in our midst who do not know the proper techniques for eating boiled crawfish. That's like New Englanders not knowing how to eat clams. To right the wrongs and spare us all from embarrassment, here are answers to crucial questions on a crucial topic — crawfish consumption.

Q: What do you do first?

A: Good question. Grasp the head of the crawfish between the same two digits on the other hand, then twist so as to break off the head cavity from the tail.

Q: Then what?

A: Suck the head.

Q: Do I have to?

A: Yes, sucking the head is probably the most important part to eating a crawfish, yet there are heathens out there who ignore this step. The head cavity contains the juices from the seasoning mixed with the fat. That's where the real flavor is. Not sucking the heads is like eating a pizza and throwing away the topping.

Q: Juices, fat, that sounds terrible.

A: It shouldn't, fat and seasoning are the essence of much cooking, such as gravies and roux. Besides, crawfish aren't very fattening anyway.

Q: How about the tail section? Is there a trick to peeling it?

A: I'm glad you asked. Of course there is. It's always easy to spot untrained crawfish eaters — they're the ones who sit there methodically peeling off the armor as though it were the skin of an orange. The right way is to merely peel off the first couple of scales from the top of the tail and then pinch the bottom, thus forcing the meat to slide out like toothpaste from a tube.

Q: What is that black strip running vertically along the tale?

A: Some people call it a vein, others refer to it as the digestive tract, which is what it really is. The most common name among crawfish connoisseurs who are too busy eating to be bothered with technicalities is the "black thing." Whatever it's called, flick it off before eating the tail.

Q: Should crawfish be eaten year-round?

A: Not really. There are some places where the mudbug is sold throughout the year, but nature knows better. By late July the crawfish armor starts turning hard as a preparation for molting. The heads, when they are firm, are more difficult to suck and the tails harder to peel. Nor is the meat as plump. Crawfish should properly be eaten in spring and early summer.

Q: How about catsup and horseradish? Should the crawfish be dipped into a mixture of the two?

A: Not if the crawfish are seasoned properly. They will have enough flavor on their own. Save the sauces for raw oysters.

Q: What if someone in Louisiana doesn't like boiled crawfish?

A: That's why there are 49 other states.

The Clover

There are some restaurants in the French Quarter known for their finer foods, others for their excellent service. Then there was the Clover Grill.

Located in the middle of the Quarter, on the corner of Bourbon and Dumaine streets, the Clover, before being taken over by new management, was an anomaly. It was not a tourist place where one could expect to find a decor of brass and eclectic furniture. There was no salad bar, and quiche and spinach salad had never crossed the counter. Instead, the Clover captured more of the charm of a truck stop. It was a slice of Airline Highway, right in the Vieux Carre.

"It's a beautiful day, Mr. Jake," a customer mused to the man behind the counter, "I think I'll go to the lake."

"You got my permission," Mr. Jake answered with a grin. "You can go to hell if you want to."

There was no phoney sentiment at the Clover Grill.

What there was was a bit of scruffiness that gave the place its unique charm. Mr. Jake presided in front of the stainless steel grill. Patrons ordered such rare delicacies as Campbell's chili con carne with toast $1.45. The decor was plain, highlighted by a photograph of Mardi Gras nuns wearing Lone Ranger masks. Color was added by pint-sized boxes of cereal stacked near the refrigerator.

There was a Times-Picayune rack at one corner of the counter, from which newspapers were sometimes shared communally. In fact, the entire grill invited a sense of community, to the extent that certain acceptable customers walked behind the counter and fixed their dishes themselves. On one typical afternoon a customer walked in and headed straight for the back room, where he grabbed an orange drink. Next, the man took two slices of bread, then went for the refrigerator where he found a Tupperware bowl filled with tuna salad. Meanwhile, another customer found his way behind the counter to pour two cups of coffee to go. But these labors provided no discount. Moments later Jake was ringing up a tuna sandwich and two cups of coffee on his cash register.

But most of the time, it was Mr. Jake behind the counter, plopping patties on the grill and dressing buns with lettuce and tomatoes In fact, burgers and fries seemed to be the staples of the Clover Grill. The burgers were adequate, but it was the fries that stood out, not so much for their flavor as for their packaging. At one point Mr. Jake had taken to sorting his fries into tiny brown paper bags. That maked the distribution more even and provided him with a **ready-made** stash when things got busy. Some people pay plenty to have pompano en papillote at the local French restaurants, whereas for a bit of change they could have pommes de terre **frites en papillote** from Mr. Jake.

"I'm getting senile," Mr. Jake joked to a female customer, "but don't laugh, one day you'll get senile too." With that bit of encouragement he took her order. Far from senile, Mr. Jake was quite spry. He moved with ease from cooking to taking orders to ringing the cash register to taking part in banter. He also acted as an unofficial welcomer. "Are you from out of town?" he once asked two women. Told that they weren't, Jake explained that had they been, he would have had a souvenir for them. The women teased for the gift anyway, prompting Mr. Jake to pull out two pairs of Bacchus beads from behind the counter.

Arthur Jacob was a retired policeman who eased into the grill business. He will be remebered, however, not for wearing a badge but for his customary white t-shirt, grey pants and large white apron. He'll also be remembered for operating a place that just oozed with a feeling of realness. The food became almost secondary to the flavor of life.

"I don't need publicity," Mr. Jake responded when told about this column. "I just operate a small neighborhood business, that's all. But I'm flattered you thought about me anyway."

With that, he walked back to the grill. Everything must have its priorities. There's no time for stardom when there are burgers to flip.

In Praise Of The Potato Poor Boy

Let us remember the forgotten foods. Some items were once popular around town but somehow faded from local menus. One is pain perdu, or lost bread, as the Americans would refer to this French dish, in which the bread was dipped into an egg and milk batter then fried. As the city became more like the mainland and less like a cultural island the dish, save for a few chefs with a memory, was lost in the land of the pancake.

Another item to suffer such a fate was calas, or rice cakes, a confection naturally sold in the port city of rice country. Mammies with red bandannas on their heads, after whom certain rag dolls would be patterned, carried baskets while hollering "calas" to the Quarter's pedestrians. These days, the Quarter's rhythm has lost one of its lyrics.

Then there is the potato poor boy, in which fries, real fries, not the frozen crinkle cut or processed fast food types, were served on a French bread loaf. Poor boys were a staple of working-class New Orleans. On good days, when there were banana boats to unload and beer to bottle, there might be enough extra change to order from the upper echelon of poor boys — the dripping roast beef or the crispy fried oyster varieties. But when times were tough, the potato poor boy at least maintained energy. In fact, in the entire spectrum of poor boys the only thing cheaper than the potato was the legendary lettuce and tomato poor boy. A worker would order that with hopes of scrounging a slice or two of luncheon meat from a cohort. Sometimes the quest would fail and the lettuce and tomato would be seasoned only by imagination — the ultimate diet.

Where the potato poor boy survives it is mostly as a curiosity, at places such as Katie's, a Mid-City neighborhood restaurant. Katie's has many star items on its menu including great onion rings, a cream of broccoli soup, good soft shell crabs and a super chef salad, but also on the menu, for those who want either to remember or to experience, is the potato poor boy.

A sandwich made with fried potatoes is bound to be a troubled dish in a health-conscious age, although there are some contradictions. While a potato poor boy seems to be a bit heavy, there is less resistance to the notion of a regular poor boy with an order of french fries on the side. With potatoes, as in politics, it is image that wins friends.

My purpose in ordering the dish was purely as research of an historic relic. In this temple, the mood was set by the sounds of idol worship as the juke box settled on Professor Longhair's "Big Chief." New Orleans rhythm and blues is the proper music for poor boy consumption.

There are other rules to potato poor boy etiquette, some of which are too often violated. There have, for example, been reports of heathens who garnish their spud sandwiches with foreign sauces such as mustard and catsup. Potato poor boy purists know that there is only one way to prepare the meal and that is with mayonnaise (Blue Plate, preferably) and then — and this is essential — roast beef gravy. The latter is a gesture rich not only in taste but in symbolism. The roast beef poor boy is the aristocrat of the sandwich line; the potato is the commoner. The mingling of the juices is in the spirit of "share the wealth:" if we can't have the meat, at least pass the gravy.

Having now had a potato poor boy I can report that it is a decent meal. It doesn't have the outright taste of a ham and cheese, oyster or hot sausage poor boy, but it does have a light, subtle flavor of its own. It was well known to people who sensed that when times were tough but the spirit high; there were ways to get along.

MUSIC

A Little Bluegrass

There are some places in this country where Bill Monroe will draw a far larger crowd than Fats Domino, But New Orleans is not one of them. Thus it happened that during the final hour of the Jazz Fest, while thousands congregated around Stage Four to hear Fats, only a few hundred gathered in front of Stage Three to listen to one of the major figures in country music. In fact, the only thing that keeps the name of Bill Monroe from being treated with the same reverence and mystique accorded to a Hank Williams or Jimmy Rogers is that Monroe, at 73, is still alive, still singin', still pickin'.

"'Foggy Mountain' — do 'Foggy Mountain'," a girl in the audience cries. Others turn the cry into a chant. Monroe hears his audience and proves to be a crowd pleaser. After a nod to the boys in his band, the fiddler starts fiddling, the guitarist and banjo player start strumming, the bass player starts thumping and Monroe — he plays the mandolin. What emerges from the combination is bluegrass music — country at its purest played by its finest, Bill Monroe and his Blue Grass Boys.

A week earlier, Frankie Ford had stood on a Jazz Fest stage and preambled his next selection by announcing that, "This next song doesn't go 'something like this,' it goes exactly like this." Then Ford launched into his hit, "Sea Cruise." So it was with Monroe. He wasn't playing a version of the country classics, he was playing the country classics as he made them famous. The crowd danced to "Foggy Mountain Breakdown," having never heard it performed better.

Monroe's importance to American music was not overstated in the Jazz Fest program. While lesser groups were given longer descriptions, the caption next to the listing of Monroe and his group said merely, "A bluegrass band." A more accurate description of him was mistakenly listed under the name of Bill Malone, a local student of country music and performer: "One of the legendary keepers of the bluegrass flame, Bill is widely considered the father of bluegrass music. One book on the subject, *Old As The Hills: The Story of Bluegrass Music*, by Steven DePrice, is a bit more generous with its praise: "Bill Monroe deserves far more than a passing mention or even several paragraphs. Quite simply, if it had not been for Bill Monroe, there might never had been bluegrass music at all."

Bluegrass evolved as a fusion of Anglo-American folk music and Southern black musical traditions — particularly the use of the guitar and fiddle—to which Monroe added the mandolin, which he transformed from a backup position to a spritely lead instrument. He took the music on the road and, through the Grand Ole Opry, made it famous.

"Hey that looks just like Bill Monroe," one passerby at the Jazz Fest said with a drawl — "There's his name on the sign — it really is Bill Monroe."

"That's the way gospel should be sung," Monroe assured the crowd after he had urged the audience to sing along during the refrains of "Swing Low Sweet Chariot," "Everybody should sing gospel together."

His was a participatory performance. Monroe asked if there was anyone in the crowd who knew how to clog dance. A short, squat woman wearing a Minnesota Twins baseball cap worked her way to the stage. Monroe took her to the side, where he began to clog (a folk dance of sorts) with her, while the Blue Grass Boys played music suitable for clogging. But the music was cut short by Monroe, who quickly realized that the woman clogged about as well as the Twins played baseball. He returned to his mandolin. The people had come to hear him play, anyway.

Both Monroe and the Boys wore suits, ties and white ten gallon hats, the uniform of old school country music, far different from the jeans and earrings of the so-called "outlaw" groups led by the likes of Willie Nelson and Waylon Jennings. But the old school sure taught people how to play country music. With the hour's performance nearly up, the group broke into a medley of five bluegrass songs that made the crowd crazy. As the Boys left the stage, the small crowd roared almost loud enough to outshout the thousands watching Fats. Monroe paused at the stage's edge. The applause increased. He raised one finger in the air as though to ask if the audience wanted one last song. The applause grew louder. But the stage manager signaled that the show must come to an end, thereby cutting short a musical upheaval. In this town of rhythm and blues and jazz, a country mandolin player had left the crowd wanting more.

Some of those who appreciated the man and his music gathered backstage while Monroe reached for extended hands. But many of those who had attended the Jazz Fest walked by, oblivious to what the commotion was all about.

They had gone to Jazz Fest in search of music at its best and not realized that that day, the top of the mountain was covered with blue grass.

Piano Player

Just when the Quarter seemed to be fatally on the skids. Just as the litter from the Pat O'Brien's cups and the flicked cigarette butts seemed about to bury the Quarter. Just as the shameless pitches from would-be auction houses and the cheap carnival atmosphere of a game room seemed to serve notice that the good guys are losing. Just when it all seemed too bad, there was Al Broussard.

As it happened, Broussard briefly added to the frustration that evening by being late. "He's never been this late before," the bartender at the tiny 711 Bar on Bourbon Street worried. "Maybe he went to see Stevie Wonder." Had Broussard done so, Stevie might have wondered how a man at 80 can look 50 and live so young. Moments later, Al

Broussard, octogenarian piano player, walked in. Why was he late? His moped broke.

Al Broussard's age is a curiosity but really only incidental to his story, a story about a musician who has never once left New Orleans and who learned his profession from fellow black piano players. He is a piano player, a performer and especially a charmer, part of the trade of the barroom pianist.

"Hi, Al," some women shout as they pass outside the front door. "Hi, ladies," Broussard answers with glee. The piano player is stationed right at the front window, perched where he can flirt with the passing crowd, drawing its members in, if not always with his smile then with his music.

That smile is infectious as Broussard aims a grin at whoever in the bar is noticing the tricks his fingers are performing on the keyboard. Leaning into the microphone, he croons the old piano bar jazz tunes, announcing to passing women, "I'm Confessing That I Love You." When the mood is right, he purses his lips to the microphone making a horn-like sound to accompany his piano playing. This is no ordinary musician; as Broussard himself announces, he is the "human trumpet."

Some of the passersby hear the trumpet's call. Two men walk in. Broussard notices their Lions International vests and, while holding his melody, asks if they had anything to do with a Lions Club building located on Rampart Street in 1926. There is probably not a Lion alive who remembers the location, including those two who, the back of their vests revealed, were from San Angelo, Texas. But the question was rhetorical anyway — Broussard talks New Orleans.

He talks romance, too, flirting with whichever woman has won his eye for the moment, flashing that overpowering grin as the sounds come out just right. "What'll it be, Chivas Regal?" a customer asks. "Johnny Walker," Broussard answers, perhaps thinking of nourishment as he breaks into boogie-woogie.

His surroundings are worn — tired more than quaint. The bar stools that front his piano are tattered, the barroom itself is barely distinguishable from the outside, an easy place to pass by. His is a simple business. He sings, people stop to listen. Most drop a bill into the tip jar as they leave. His piano top is the marketing center of his auxiliary enterprises, consisting of one cassette and one album. Besides that, he simply makes music and smiles.

Somewhere along the Quarter's streets, there are musicians who draw larger crowds but who smile less; somewhere other musicians who have not gotten the attention they deserve don't smile at all anymore. Probably none of them will still be playing when they're 80. But Al Broussard still is, and as long as Bourbon Street hears his songs, there may be hope that the good guys will win after all.

The Dirty Dozen At The Blue Room

What has to be understood is what going to the "Blue Room" has meant in the city's social history. The Room was the place, stepping out at its highest, the special occasion rendezvous for the most special of occasions. It was the spot where bonafide stars would perform for the conventioneers, the lovestruck and the politicians who came in from out of the lobby.

It is the place memorialized in a thousand hope chests around the city either by an autographed menu from some distant evening or by a faded matchbook with a scratchy photo pasted on the inside. Many of the yellowing pictures of celebrities that hang on business district restaurant walls no doubt can be traced back to performers playing the Room. They talk of the old days. Joe E. Lewis, Jimmy Durante, Phil Harris, Glenn Miller, Guy Lombardo, they all played the Room. More recently Tina Turner, on the eve of her rediscovery, sang and privately danced for the Room's audience. This was the place of stars, both coming and going.

That's why there seemed to be something especially touching last week when the featured act was the Dirty Dozen Brass Band. This group has played New Orleans before — in its streets, in the bars, in smokey neighborhood night spots. There are eight, not twelve, members of the Dirty Dozen, and they are all from and about New Orleans.

Their music is a fusion of Dixieland and progressive jazz. The Dozen, after all, are young men who want to make their own statement. But when they walk on the stage and open with spirited whistling accompanying an upbeat "Big Chief," it is obvious that these guys were raised in a setting where jazz, rhythm and blues, and Mardi Gras Indian lore created a fusion of their own. That's a sound that belongs to only one city.

Since 1917, when Nick LaRocca brought a jazz band north to make the first jazz record, there has been a parade of New Orleans-bred musicians to popularize the city's musical reputation throughout the world. Consider the names: Armstrong, Prima, Fountain, Hirt, the Dukes of Dixieland, the Marsalises, and now the newest, the Dirty Dozen.

Their mission has already begun. Prior to the Blue Room the group had played the Bar Lionel Hampton at Paris' Meridien, a hot spot for sophisticated jazz. Jazz bands from the states are common there but not bands raised on Bourbon Street parades and who can whistle to Professor Longhair. In the international language of jazz, New Orleans is a Babel but whose music is a faint dialect. The Dozen are jazz linguists who know how to speak out.

Their act still needs touching up, particulary as they expand beyond jazz clubs. They need more communication with audiences, especially those that know less about their music. Their staging could be better polished. But when it comes to music the Dozen are ready.

They made quite a sight, resplendent in their tuxedos and white spats, performing on that stage that has seen many great bands. The Dirty Dozen have talent, and if they get the breaks they can go far. But if symbolic victories mean anything they can already take solace that regardless of what will follow, they made it to the Blue Room.

A Hard Day's Night

There was so much excitement at City Park stadium that night that the slightest movement would be answered with screams. Thus, when workmen walked on the stage — constructed in the end zone of the open end of the horseshoe shaped stadium — people yelped, then drooled, especially as they spotted the guitars being put in place. The people in the crowd became downright ecstatic as the drum set was positioned — especially once they spotted the word "Beatles."

That happened September 16, 1964, when thanks to an adventurous disc jockey named Herb Holliday, who was willing to take the risk as a promoter, New Orleans was one of the stops on the Beatles' first visit to the New World.

In those days before the Superdome, City Park stadium was the chosen site, which means that Holliday would have taken a bath had there been a storm. But, as it turned out, the only thunder that night was from the thousands of teeny-boppers who packed the old stadium.

Some had waited in line all day, just to be first to be within the same confines as the air that the Beatles would breathe. Once the show began they waited longer while the warm-up act performed. That act was Jackie DeShannon, a rock and roller who, in those days when the teenagers were starting to hear more about a place called Viet Nam, had a melancholy hit called "What the World Needs Now is Love."

What the world, or at least the parcel of it within City Park stadium, needed that night was less love and more police. It began the instant the Beatles reached the stage — swooning teenage girls — hundreds of them — leaped the rails and began charging the stage, like Cupid's arrows flying towards a heart.

That moment should go down in history as one of the most trying for the New Orleans Police Department. On the field where high school football teams normally battled each other, New Orleans' finest blocked and tackled an opposition whose worst crimes were indeed of the heart. The field was scatterd with craziness — steady cops dragging and pulling crazed girls back to their seats.

That craziness continued throughout the following weeks. News surfaced that the Beatles' secret hideaway while they were in town was the Congress Inn, a now defunct motel, located way out on the Chef Menteur Highway — away, it was hoped, from the swooners who might not know their way to the city's outback. A rock station would give away as prizes patches of the sheets upon which the Beatles slumbered.

Then there was a local record that told the tale of a girl who happened to wander that evening past the spot where the Beatles were waiting in their limousine. The tale reached a crescendo when one of the Beatles spotted her and spoke the immortal words, "Hi bird."

As for the quality of the group's performance that night, who knows? It competed not only with the open air but with the screams. Their stage presence could not compare with for the activity on the field. The Beatles, that evening, were in effect the background band for a circus.

In the years to follow, international events would make Jackie DeShannon's plea for more love in the world more relevant, especially to that age group in attendance. Both the Beatles and their followers would become increasingly serious. But that night in New Orleans, things were just zany and happy. To a thousand or so local teenagers, that's the way life, up to that point, had seemed to be.

EXPERIENCES

The City's Hat

One summer afternoon I was walking through the Quarter when a man approached me and said he liked my hat. I explained that it was a Panama hat from Meyer the Hatter. "I know," he responded. "I'm Meyer."

These are the days for Panama hats, the time of the year when the local weather is sometimes at its most intolerable — an angry sun staring through a layer of humidity. It is the weather of the semi-tropics, a region that has created a male fashion of white cotton or seersucker suits topped by one of the best uses ever created for straw, the Panama hat.

Such hats are the authentic headpiece of the New Orleans summer, providing slight shade for those left behind to care for a city that people traditionally abandon during the warm days. These hats were worn by merchants watching their coffee being unloaded, bankers making the mid-afternoon rush to the club and ward bosses working the homes along the banana tree-shaded sidewalks.

There is a correlation — Panama hats belong in the sorts of places where banana trees grow wild. Such places are where it is alternately hot and rainy. The hats can't do much for the rain other than lose their form to it, but their wide brims block the sun's rays and their light-woven patterns keep heads cool.

These services are lost to many contemporary heads because Panama hats just aren't as commonly worn anymore. Being hatless has become more fashionable. But when they are worn they somehow make a statement, though none so boldly as did my very first Panama hat on its last ride.

I was on the train from Chicago to New Orleans. (Surely statistics would prove that people who like Panama hats are also more inclined to like trains.) As the Pullman car rushed past Ponchatoula it was time to start packing. Losing an object in a Pullman car is like misplacing something in a thimble. There is hardly any room for something to get lost. But the hat was missing.

As the train raced along Lake Pontchartrain the searching continued. No hat. Finally, with the city skyline in sight the steward joined the search. He looked in, out, up and down and then paused as though he had a nervous thought. Reluctantly, he positioned his small step ladder and then climbed to a spot where he could lower the bed, which during the daylight hours could be pushed up to a location flush with the ceiling. He pulled the bed down — we stared, he sobbed. There on one corner was the world's first straw tortilla.

As the train pulled into Union Station, the steward continued to apologize, even after my assurances that that wasn't necessary. Somehow, the hat's end seemed appropriate, at least in a symbolic way. It was, after all, Labor Day — the end of summer and the end of the hat's season. After all, having beaten the heat and never fallen victim to the rain, what could be a more appropriate ending for the hat than to meet its fate in a train called The Panama Limited?

A Dime's Worth Of Difference

A group of shoppers gathered on a corner of the Bourbon Street end of Woolworth's. They had been given tickets to a free demonstration at which, the p.a. announcement kept reminding them, they could receive free valuable prizes.

And receive prizes they did: a telephone pen holder, a telephone pen (complete with a rounded end suitable for dialing), and other treasures. By the time it was over, five of the shoppers even left with a bag filled with what was said to be $44 worth of gifts. They were the lucky ones, so lucky that in their ecstasy they probably didn't stop to think that their luck had cost them $15 they probably hadn't intended to spend. Somehow that lumpy looking dime store pitch man with the Hawaiian wedding shirt had made them feel like they had a bargain, and bargains, of course, are what dime stores are all about.

There are only three downtown dime stores left now since Kress closed last year. But the three survivors, two Woolworth's and a McCrory's, are still very much alive, with a bazaar-like atmosphere. Actually, dime stores, especially the bigger urban business district ones, are the carnivals of retail. The side shows, the super deals, even the popcorn and peanuts are all there. The p.a. system chatters with "unadvertised specials" now going on, "at this very minute" — a pitch to cash in on the rare good fortune of being in the right place at the right time.

At the Bourbon-and-Canal Woolworth's the carnival air is more pronounced because of the extra tourist trade. The store has an entire corner dedicated to souvenirs, like gigantic cigars with Bourbon Street labels ("made with real tobacco") or a snow globe that one can shake to see what the St. Louis Cathedral looks like after a blizzard.

There are some people who might consider such items a bit tacky, but dime stores have their own standards. McCrory's, for example, is the place to shop if you're a connoisseur of fine black velvet paintings just like those sold from trucks alongside highways. These come in various dimensions, including the coveted sofa size. The upper walls along the back and side of the store are lined with the paintings. There's Elvis in shades of yellow and blue, singing his heart out on a black velvet background. Another shows a truck enlightened by a beam from heaven. Not all the paintings are serious, however; there's one with the Road Runner beeping down a black velvet highway.

As in all art, some license is needed. One painting was of a panther. Since panthers are black, the background was compromised to create a rare pink velvet painting.

If there is one subject that dominates the design in dime stores these days, however, it is Pac Man. The glorified yellow dot adorns jackets, t-shirts, puzzles, games, and lunch boxes, and is even sold as a puppet. Move over, Snoopy, this is the computer age. Dime stores keep up with the trends as faithfully as they hype the bargains. .

One is tempted to dismiss the store goods as cheap, low-quality. But for everyday items — shampoos, soaps, plastic coat hangers — the stores are a decent place to shop. Even though the term "dime store" has long been archaic, the prices generally are good and the inventories are large. The Woolworth's at the corner of Canal and Rampart even has two floors worth of stuff.

Like shopping centers, dime stores feed hungry shoppers. The stand-up lunch counters invariably feature hot dogs, a meat loaf special, and a hoagie, but there are also super lunch counters, like the one at the Rampart Woolworth's. The serving area is enormous, stretching across the width of the store, with counters jutting out like piers in a harbor. There is probably no commercial eatery in New Orleans that serves so many lunches in one day.

Showing my stuff as a participatory journalist, I experienced one of those lunches. It was a tough decision between the Steak-umm sandwich and something called a Duke of Rib platter. I opted for the latter because it was the day's special and I, too, wanted to feel like I had a bargain. The Duke wasn't bad but the ambiance was even better. Across from me was a tyke playing with his food. The lettering on his red baseball cap read: "Only the good die young; I'll be here forever." Meanwhile, the guy sitting next to me had been eyeing my Duke of Rib and decided that was what he wanted also. The waitress, while writing my tab, told how on the day before someone had pasted the number from the corner of a $10 bill over the edge of a one and tried to pass the bill off for the higher value. The guy next to me was unimpressed, explaining, in an obvious Yankee dialect, that that stunt was pulled "all the time" in New York, only they doctor the bills there to look like 20s. One does not learn those sorts of things lunching at Galatoire's.

What one does learn at the dime stores is the spirit of commercialism, the sales technique, the mass marketing created by the assembly line, the lure of the deal.

I was reminded about the latter one evening later while I was walking down Canal Street. A man who was waiting for a bus looked familiar. He was a bit lumpy and was wearing a Hawaiian wedding shirt. It was the dime store sales pitchman. As he waited he began chatting with a woman next to him. Little did the lady realize that by the time her wait ended she might buy the bus.

Big Bird For A Day

It was one of those moments when I was starting to feel incredibly silly, especially as I pulled up the bright yellow tights then stepped into the fuzzy yellow feet.

Through a curious set of circumstances I had somehow been recruited to assume the role of something resembling Big Bird, the star of Sesame Street, for WYES-TV's 25th anniversary party. It was not a role that I relished, particularly as I placed on the huge headpiece, which must have added an extra 20 degrees to an already hot day. But there I was, plopping down the hall, like a siliconed chicken, alongside Nick, who had been drafted to be Cookie Monster.

We were escorted to a corner of the main studio where we were seated so that the kiddies could shake our hands and receive balloons. Here I learned one law of ornithology that had somehow escaped me: because of their huge lumpy mitts, Big Birds cannot easily hand out balloons. Manual dexterity is lost, which may explain why there are no famous Big Bird baseball pitchers or piano players. Cookie Monster had to handle most of the balloon-giving chores.

My vision was through the wire mesh beneath the beak, which meant that I was seeing the world not through Big Bird's eyes but rather his mouth. Through that mouth I saw wide-eyed kids who were enthralled by seeing their first celebrity.

I'll have to admit that I accepted my role despite an initial W.C. Fields type attitude towards kids. But those who came to see Big Bird that day were charming. They were also an easy audience. They knew, of course, that there was a person in that costume, but that wasn't standing in the way of their fantasy. They asked questions, and giggled incessantly at any meager attempt at humor.

When Cookie Monster began groaning for more cookies, that prompted one girl to ask Big Bird what he ate. "Bird seeds," I answered. "Bird seeds," she replied. Giggle, giggle, giggle.

"How did you get here?" one asked. "I flew," Big Bird answered. "With your wings?" "No, in an airplane." The notion of this feathery creature in a 727 was too much. More giggles.

"Has Zero left for the South Pole yet?" someone asked. "Zero? South Pole?" I thought in a mild panic. Then I remembered. Fortunately, I had prepared for my role by watching "Sesame Street" that morning. One episode had Big Bird's cousin, a penguin named Zero, about to head back home. "Yeah, he left," I answered. "Are you going to go see him?" "No," I replied, "it's too cold over there." Giggle, giggle.

One boy was especially inquisitive; he wanted to know where Sesame Street was located. I recalled having heard once that the street was patterned after a block in Harlem, so I answered, "In New York." "In New York!" the boy shot back seeming astonished. He wasn't giggling. I think he wanted me to say that Sesame Street was either next door or at least in the mall at Lakeside Shopping Center. Undaunted, he double-checked with Cookie Monster. "Where's Sesame Street?" Cookie answered: "On television." The boy seemed satisfied.

Television was obviously a better place to be from than New York.

At intervals I was escorted outside where adults and more kids were picnicking and listening to the Dukes of Dixieland. Here I learned a sociology lession. When one is bright yellow, feathery and about seven feet tall he tends to stand out in a crowd. Periodically I was stopped to pose for a picture. My vision was limited, so I could only sense that some tyke was standing next to me while some parent was aiming his Instamatic. Dutifully I waved at the camera as though I knew what was going on.

My one initiative was when I left my escort, stepped through the crowd, which was sprawled on the lawn, and shook hands with one of the Dukes while he was playing. "It's Big Bird!" the Duke announced over the microphone. The crowd applauded and I waved and did an impromptu jig. In street clothes I would have been sitting quietly in the back of the crowd; suddenly the costume was making me feel bold. Big Bird can do no wrong.

I sensed that assuredness, particulary back in the studio, as a cult seemed to form around Big and Cookie. A few kids spent their afternoon in our presence, just staring and asking questions. When the escort took my sidekick, Cookie Monster, outside, one boy even climbed in Cookie's chair and sat quietly, just to be sure that Big Bird wouldn't be left alone.

It was a rare experience. For three hours I was able to be the soul of a perfectly lovable character, one neutered of any prejudices of sex or race. Everyone loves a big cuddly critter, although a few of the kids were at an age where they could barely hang on to that affection and still make it believable.

Three girls, for example, were standing in front of me, discussing which of the various broadcast times they watched "Sesame Street." "I watch it at one each afternoon," one girl explained, "right after 'All My Children'." Sad for the Big Birds of the world that there comes a time when people grow up.

Lighting My Fire

This was a two-match year. That's a bit dissappointing, coming after last year's phenomenal performance when it only took me one match to light the floor furnace. But once a person has acheived something that cannot possibly be improved on, he has to accept doing worse.

I might have done it with a single match this year had I had long kitchen matches instead of paper ones. The little match just couldn't last long enough, given the strain of being lowered by its feet with a flame at its head towards the pilot. A sudden gust from beneath the house extinguished it an instant before ignition.

Two matches to light a floor furnace is no disgrace, however, especially given those first few years when lighting the furnace helped support the Plaquemines Parish sulphur industry. Those were the years when a plumber had to crawl beneath the house to spot the various places where dogs had nibbled on the line connecting the thermostat or where an innocent valve would require $65 worth of labor to be changed.

But it was all worth it, because there is nothing quite like a floor furnace. Indeed, people may be attracted to old houses by the fireplaces, but it's the floor furnaces that get the job done. Heat can come in various forms but in no way does warmth become so titillating as when it rises from the floor, gently climbing the legs.

People have been known to fight for the right to stand over the floor furnace grate for quick warming from the bottom up. When the plumber finally lit the heater on that cold January day a few years ago, we collided trying to be the first to straddle the furnace. Because of my long-standing policy of never getting into a shoving match with a man carrying a monkey wrench, I acquiesced and watched the ecstasy as his frostbitten snarl from tooling about in the frigid underside of the house gave way to a glow. Meanwhile, I wrote out the check to pay for his smile.

This is the time of the year when furnaces are being lit for the winter. There are a couple of techniques to be aware of. One is that there is a right way, which consists of attaching the match to the rod that the company supplied when the heater was installed, then carefully reading the instructions next to the lever which controls the gas. That's the right way. But since most floor furnaces are old, the rods are usually long gone, necessitating the use of a straightened coat hanger with a loop twisted at the end. Of course, the instructions are usually worn away, so lighting the heater really consists of lowering a makeshift rod with a match hanging to it while arbitrarily twisting and pushing the lever.

When the pilot ignites, winter is half saved, the other half comes when the thermostat is switched on and the full furnace lights. That is the crucial moment. In fact, it is one of the celebrated moments of the entire calendar year. Dust never has a more glorious moment than when it burns as a sacrifice to the newly-lit furnace. Forget about pumpkin pies and hot apple cider—the real smell of the coming of winter is that of dust as it sizzles.

Another smell of the season's arrival is singed trouser legs and branded soles. You can tell a New Orleanian who lives in an old house, he's the one with grate marks on the bottom of his shoes.

Floor furnaces, of course, do have their drawbacks; they chug-a-lug lots of fuel, they eliminate valuable floor space, and their heating is spotty, failing to fully saturate distant corners. Still, pity those with temperature controlled totally electric housing, where the heat is uniform all winter. They are denied the experience of realizing that getting warm can feel so good.

Instant New Orleans

Admittedly, I was biased as I entered the new Esplanade Mall shopping center in Kenner. I had already decided that I didn't like the notion of instant New Orleans created on the plains of Kenner. It is bad enough that the shopping center is located at the end of West Esplanade Boulevard, as though it is an extension of the old Creole trail from the French Quarter to Bayou St. John, but then to design the complex with a New Orleans motif seems an identity rip-off.

Some might consider it flattery instead, but I'm one of those people doomed to thinking of things in political terms to whom suburbanization has not set well. As a piece of architecture, the Esplanade Mall is respectable, and its attempts at a New Orleans look are far more imaginative than the joints around Fat City that hang a false balcony on a cheap store front and give it a Vieux Carre name. But there is something that stabs at local pride upon seeing a Cafe Du Monde stand in the middle of a suburban shopping center. Perhaps that is the next step of suburbanization. First the flight, then the replication, preserved in an antiseptic way — old town under glass.

Flight of a different sort, incidentally, brings to mind another criticism of the mall. Kenner is a city with its own history, its own story to tell. It was the site of a sugar cane plantation and then a home for Sicilian truck farmers. Aviation is certainly more a part of the airport city's history than any town in the state. Perhaps its history is overshadowed by New Orleans', but wouldn't it have been more interesting and innovative if the center's design had been a reflection of Kenner? Instead, there is a colony mentality in the design.

None of this matters very much except for those of us who worry about the generations raised, schooled and cared for in the suburbs, who will best know New Orleans from the perspective of a suburban shopping center. They may never fully appreciate that only about 15 miles to the east there is a real Esplanade and a real Quarter with sights, sounds and smells that are genuine. There are magnolia trees and busy neighborhoods, some with music filling the street. There are dangers too, but that comes with life in an environment that is not controlled. That same environment also produces originality. Real life has its trade-outs.

As fate would have it, that same evening I heard Irma Thomas at the 601 Club near the warehouse district. Fate knew what it was doing. After my afternoon in Kenner I had a real need to be on Tchoupitoulas Street, listening to New Orleans rhythm and blues. Thomas was great, singing the old ones, the songs that flowered in the central city black neighborhoods and became a suburban generation's nostalgia. Some of the songs could have come out of any big city that has a feeling for the blues, but when Irma began belting "Jock-a-Mo," she was delivering a fusion of R&B and Mardi Gras Indian chant that is solely and soulfully New Orleans.

In other cities, people may dance to the music of their native states, but along Tchoupitoulas Street they were waving hankerchiefs and second-lining to Irma. Somehow the experience made me feel better about the mall where, rumor has it, one of the stores will be decorated in purple, green and gold — Mardi Gras colors. With paint and building materials it is possible to recreate a particular look, but as I watched the second line on Tchoupitoulas Street I felt satisfied that there will always be a sense of place that just does not cross parish lines.

THE QUARTER

His New Orleans

In a scene from "A Streetcar Named Desire" Blanche DuBois and Mitch, a card-playing buddy of Stanley Kowalski's, are sitting outside on a steamy New Orleans night just moments after Stanley has thrown one of his tantrums. Blanche suddenly realizes that she is wearing only a light robe and thus proclaims with Southern ladylike indignity, "I'm not properly dressed." Mitch consoles her by assuring, "That don't make no difference in the Quarter."

Tennessee Williams' legacy has found new life over the last week. As T.E. Kalem wrote of Williams in *Time*, "A great artist is reborn at the hour of his death." Much of that rebirth has consisted of discussion about his life and work; I have also wondered about the New Orleans, or at least the portion of it in the vicinity of the French Quarter, that he wrote about. How different is it from the place where Mitch and Blanche, through the playwright's eyes, held each other?

Certainly the Quarter has changed, as it must, although for many who knew his plays Williams'scenes are set amidst such change. The author described a Quarter that had already undergone generations of change and at the time of his plays that change was still in motion. Even where there is an attempt to preserve the past, change is constant. There are no Italian women peddling flowers along the street anymore, and there's no streetcar clanging its way to and around the Quarter.

Moreover, the automobile, whose popularization was partially responsible for the removal of the Desire streetcar, would likely have allowed Stanley and his wife Stella to move from the vicinity of the Quarter to the open spaces of Marrero, Kenner or Westwego — places near the bowling alleys. Those without cars might have to depend on a bus named Desire. Over the years, the neighbors would have changed. Instead of fellow poker players Stanley, had he stayed, would have seen white-collar types gutting the old buildings for restoration. The neighborhood which Stanley might have thought of as being simply "near the Quarter" suddenly would be referred to as "The Faubourg Marigny" — a name that in itself would seem to drive up rents. Stanley, philosopher that he was, would pronounce to Stella, as decades of other Quarter residents had announced to their companions, "The Quarter isn't what it used to be."

Nor would those in search of Williams' French Quarter find the area to be the impressionistic scene of shadows, palms and whirling ceiling fans depicted in the play. At some old haunts, the jazz beat has even been replaced by the programmed bugling of a Pac Man machine.

But within that change much of the character is still there, as is a new generation of characters. The Quarter is still a bohemian sort of place, filled with people who would share Blanche's admission that. "I don't want realism; I want magic." Musicians work the streets; artists tote their canvases; old ladies with head scarves wander, seemingly in circles; writers search for inspiration; neighbors sit on the stoops and laugh with each other; strangers make liaisons on the corners; men embrace each other and visitors gawk.

That sense of fatalism is still there, too. . . not over yellow fever or Kentuckians or Italians as in the past, but because of traffic, tourism, a recession. Among the carefree of the Quarter the sense of doom has always been pervasive — only the causes have changed.

Williams would likely have thought that the modern-day differences in the Quarter are merely cosmetic, and that the characters and passions that inspire great plays are still there. His friends report that on his return visits he tried to discover those players and feelings, or at the very least tried to parody them. As one story goes, admirers would occasionally have a drink sent to him while he dined at Marti's restaurant near his home. On at least one occasion Williams, before leaving the restaurant, went to the person who sent the drink, thanked him, paused, then added, in a Blanche-like drawl, "I always depend on the kindness of strangers."

That said, he would leave, sometimes to walk the streets of the Quarter. Nearby was a New Orleans of skyscrapers, interstates and shopping centers that he never saw. He was too busy looking for magic.

An Overture

As the story goes, in 1821 Nicholas Girod, a former mayor of New Orleans, offered his home to the deposed emperor Napoleon, who was in exile in St. Helena. The little general, however, never made the move, having died before it could be considered.

From a selfish standpoint, it is probably better for the Quarter that Napoleon never came to New Orleans; otherwise the building where he would have lived would now be a cold museum. Without his prescence, but with his name, the Napoleon House thrives instead as one of the most intriguing lunch spots and bars in the city.

It is a place that is clearly in a time warp, having survived at different times the coming of Americans, pirates and tourists. Somehow it remains a locals' place, though with something of a bohemian coffee shop atmosphere. It is a place that follows its own calendar.

"Summer Lunch Specials," the menu advertises, oblivious to the fact that to everyone else it is still winter. The specials don't matter much, for the regular items mean most on the menu — the splendid muffaletta or the meatball with mozzarella sandwiches (both legacies from yet another invasion — that of the Italians). To chase it, there is the house special, the Pimm's cup drink, which mixes Pimm's liquor and lemonade and is served, not in a cup, but in a tall glass with a cucumber slice floating in the middle. "It's refreshing," the waiter assures, in apparent reference to the house's make-believe summer.

And refreshing it was as I recalled one night during the real summer past when the air was New Orleans sticky. The Pimm's cup seemed perfect that evening in the patio as the fireworks from the World's Fair could be heard ricocheting above.

There was the sense of fireworks on my last visit, too, but it was because of a recording of "The 1812 Overture" reached a crescendo. Tchaikovsky would have never known it, but his piece was perfect for the Napoleon House, not only because it was dedicated to Napoleon, but because 1812 also happened to be the year that Girod began his three-year stint as mayor. One wonders if His Honor was peeping at Maspero's across the street in 1814, when Andrew Jackson met with the Lafitte brothers to plan the defense of New Orleans from the oncoming British. What a combination they would have made sitting in Girod's patio sipping a Pimm's cup — a mayor, a general and two pirates.

These days, the activity at the Napoleon House is less dramatic. Instead of history being written there, grafitti is scrawled on the walls, but the messages are passive (Joe Loves Jane, Hugo Loves Bob), befitting a place that boasts of playing classical music only.

It is music that sets a mood. A piano concerto is highlighted by the drizzle outside and the swish of tires on the wet street. A saxophone sings from somewhere along the street.

It's enough to give one pause to realize that Napoleon's life was one of mixed accomplishments — one in which he conquered Europe but was denied experiencing the corner of Chartres and St. Louis.

Following Kate

Kate was back to work walking the streets of the Quarter. Each evening she makes her rounds beginning on Chartres then over to Esplanade, down Royal, across Bourbon, through the crowds. Some passersby will stare at Kate, but no one would dare stand in her way, for Kate is a driven woman.

On this evening she was driven by Bob, a burly man with a totally bald head, a bit of a goatee and an earring on one lobe. Bob spoke with a bit of an Eastern twang as he steered the buggy, his narration with an occasional "Giddyup Kate."

Locals hardly ever ride those buggies that tour the Quarter, and thus miss the perspective of tourguides whose job qualifications include the ability to handle a mule. "That's Tujague's, the second-oldest family-owned restaurant in New Orleans," Bob explained as Kate drew the buggy past the Creole restaurant. "What type of food do they serve?" a Chinese gentleman in the front seat asked. "Spanish," Bob answered with authority. "Giddyup Kate."

After having shown his passengers what now passes as the original Streetcar Named Desire parked in back of the Mint, Bob brought his vehicle to a halt alongside the Lalurie mansion. The macabre legends attached to this building, embellished with references to tortured slaves, a mad madame and their ghosts that spook the roof, are a natural for tourguides. This night the story was made lively by a guy with long hair who happened to be walking by. As Bob spoke, the streetwalker began making ghost sounds. "Do you live there?" one of the passengers asked. "No, I died there," he answered, then flitted away. "Giddyup Kate."

If the ghosts of Buddy Bolden, Bunk Johnson or Louis Armstrong were around that night they might have been surprised to hear that Preservation Hall was where jazz was started. Surprisingly, Bob did not offer the exact time and date on which the music began.

There were more surprises, particularly as the buggy passed Maspero's Slave Exchange, to which, Bob explained, connecting tunnels were built from the river. The tunnels were built so that the slaves would not have to walk the streets to get to the exchange. Those slave exchangers must have really been compassionate.

Mayor Nicholas Girod had had some compassion for Napoleon and because of that he had engaged in some loose talk in which his home could conceivably be used as a refuge for the then deposed emperor. From then on the building would come to be known as the Napoleon House in honor of a plan that never got past the planning stage. But as Bob told it the governor of Louisiana had sent ships to rescue the emperor who died shortly before they arrived. Based on that information might we assume that that was the beginning of the Louisiana Navy, which could account for the state placing a river alongside the city's edge.

During the half hour Bob had provided a constant flow of information of which far more was right than wrong. He was particularly expert at the things that counted the most — the best restaurants, the places that were too expensive, a good spot for a daiquiri. He even noted a bikers' bar.

As for the history, it was no more misleading than most of the other legends that are inevitable in an old town. The casual tourist really wants nothing more than fantasy, and that's what they got.

But the narration was secondary to the ride itself. It must be reported that the Quarter takes on a different feel when seen from a buggy. The isolation of the automobile is removed. The view is set back from the closeness of the pedestrian's sidewalk. The open air allows for more of the feel and smell of the Quarter. Places I have driven by all my life seemed to dazzle a bit more.

But even dazzle must come to an end as Bob helped his passengers off the buggy. It would soon be time for Kate to begin again her trek, along which there were more stories to be told, and more history to be created.

The First Days

On the Monday before its Saturday opening the Jax Brewery development seemed nowhere near ready. Paint cans blocked the stairways, construction workers bumped into each other, counters were topped with drills and sawdust and there was no sign of inventory, no evidence that within five days delicate merchandise and spicy food would be marketed from behind those counters. On the Monday before its opening the Jax Brewery might have seemed to be heading for an opening day fiasco.

Might have, but not really, not to anyone who remembered the World's Fair site on the day before it opened. Paint cans lined the streets; construction workers bumped into each other. By comparison, for the workers at Jax to accomplish a month's worth of work in a week seemed easy.

"We've come a long way since Monday," Jax developer Darryl Berger said while beaming during the renovated brewery's first Sunday afternoon. People were still bumping into each other but this time they were customers inspecting the chrome and glass meant to give part of the brewery a modern look or glancing at the tile and pressed tin ceilings intended to provide a feeling of instant antiquity. They may have been dazzled by an overload of styles, if they weren't already dazzled by the sense of discovery somewhat akin to the opening days of the fair when there was that sense of being somewhere else but in your own town.

That dazzle was infectious on that Sunday, a day which tends to be the Quarter's best, in October, perhaps the city's best month. There is a rule of elasticity in New Orleans which mandates that all conceivable advancements must be accompanied by the past. Thus it is that grand openings are accompanied by jazz bands, and thus it was that several blocks away, on the corner of Decatur and Ursulines, Irma Thomas included in her repertoire some of the old songs that the boys in the Jax bottle shop must have hummed back in the days when those in the building spoke of conveyor rather than designer belts.

Not connected to the opening but no less a part of the color was a drag costume contest further down on Decatur Street in which a sultry figure in leopard skin, identified as Wilma Flintstone, beat out for first place two bearded guys in tutus and wigs claiming to be the World's Fairies. Even in their outrageousness some of the contestants could not overlook the specter of the brewery which drew them to finish their evening by munching on croissants at the brewery's outdoor cafe. The boys in the brewhouse might have been less tolerant of the guys in drag, but at the new improved brewery the masqueraders were just another bit of local color reflecting the spirit in the Quarter that night.

Most of that spirit was in the vicinity of Jackson Square, where businesses will no doubt profit the most from the brewery. New shops in the old Pontalba buildings were being readied and those customers from the audience at Le Petit Theatre discovered that they now had a nearby spot for after the show.

Every action, so we are told, creates an opposite reaction, and there will no doubt be businesses in the Quarter to suffer from the opening of the brewery. They will be the weak, made extinct by the ruthlessness of economic Darwinism in much the same way that national breweries crushed the little brewhouse that once was Jax.

As fate had it that demise was merely the pattern common among urban riverfronts: less manufacturing and more retail; less grease, more glitz. It's a pattern that will be continued in New Orleans and in other cities, but on that October evening as the fireworks from the nearby World's Fair illuminated the sparkling brewery, all that seemed to matter was that Jax had not only gracefully survived its inauguration, but was now the jewel of the riverfront.

Goodbye, North Rampart

This is the last issue of Gambit published from 840 North Rampart. We'll be moving to the Maison Blanche Building. Our stay at this location has been brief, a year exactly, but long enough to give a feel for the special building we've occupied, and a special street, North Rampart.

In a way, I feel like Gambit belongs in this little building on the corner of Rampart and Dumaine. It was once the home of Cosimo Matassa's J&M Recording Studio, the place where New Orleans' rhythm and blues was born. The Gambits of the past year were pasted up in the same tiny room where Little Richard, Fats Domino, and Ernie K-Doe made their first records.

There's a certain kinship beween Matassa's studio and Gambit, small struggling enterprises that tried to make their voices heard. From the same spot where Fats boomed into the microphone came editorials decrying the rise in utility rates; where singers hit notes, Gambit kept notes, and both the singers and the writers celebrated life in the city.

As for Rampart Street, it is one place that lives up to its reputation. Don't be concerned that the Quarter's vitality has been compromised to tourism; the free spirit still wanders uninhibited along North Rampart.

And what free spirits they are: drag queens, business people, waiters, school kids, social workers, pickpockets, cops. All are part of the pageant of Rampart which includes flambeaux and floats turning towards the auditorium, as well as dandies in tuxedos and their ladies on the way to the ball. Nothing can be quite normal on Rampart. Armstrong Park is both passive recreation and political turmoil. But then, few streets have patron saints. People worship Tennessee Williams along Rampart, in the vicinity of Marti's, where the playwright often sat on the balcony, sipping wine while watching the New Orleans he wanted to remember.

Williams would have appreciated the characters who walked through our doors. The "Button Lady" frequently stopped by to inquire if anyone was in need of lucky beans, but the *Gambit* staff proved to be a poor lot of customers for her merchandise.

Then there was the steak salesman from Kenner who explained that because his company had a surplus of steaks he had ventured to our street to offer us prices. There were takers, but the meat was tough. In fact, the boat to Kenner must have been overloaded to the rail because other merchants from that city also worked Rampart. One day we were invited to invest in surplus purses and then, later that same afternoon, surplus art. Neither vendor won customers. However, one vendor barely withstood a hard pitch to buy an ad in Gambit. That day is memorable because it was topped off by a character dressed something like Bozo the Clown, walking through the door to deliver a bottle of champagne attached to a string of balloons.

Tennessee Williams might have also enjoyed the ongoing drama called "Beat the Car Pound," played daily by workers and residents along the block. The words "tow truck" vibrate along Rampart like the chatter of a baboon warning his tribe that the lion is in sight. There is also a more silent enemy. While the tow truck's rumble, like the lion's roar, signals its coming, the meter maid, like the sullen leopard, silently patrols the sidewalk writing tickets with dizzying speed, leaving a mark on her prey. Life on Rampart has its dangers — but it's a life worth living.

In our new home, seven floors will separate us from the comedy of street life. But in exchange we will get a new view, from above, looking out — and more space. Newspapers, like all beasts, must either grow or die. As we grow, our vantage point inevitably changes.

But even from the best of vantage points one cannot see the mystical. After we move, we'll remember that down there, to the west, the freewheeling spirit of North Rampart survives.

HISTORY

A City That Was

If you've ever heard of Washington, Louisiana, then there's a lesson to be learned from it about the fate of some cities.

Washington had its day. That day began in the mid-1700s, when the St. Landry Parish town in southwest Louisiana was founded as a port along Bayou Courtableau. Lumber shipped through the port was used in what would be many of the state's historic mansions. But one of the biggest commodities was travelers who, during the steamboat age, began the trip west from New Orleans along an intricate system of bayous to Washington, which was the southwestern terminus for Wells Fargo. As Washington became a major port, and as the Spanish hotel flourished, the town became the state's gateway to the West.

Washington might have continued to grow were it not for the floodwaters of technology. In 1882 the Texas and Pacific Railroad laid a track across southern Louisiana, a track six miles to the south. Soon farmers and lumbermen were discovering that it was cheaper and quicker to shop by railroad. The commercial activity moved towards the tracks. Opelousas, the home of Jim Bowie, got the business, while Washington got the knife. The trains made previous forms of travel obsolete, The steamboats left, the hotel closed, the people moved. New railroad towns, such as Crowley, Jennings and Eunice, would emerge, old steamboatin' towns would shrivel. Modern times were cruel.

Washington's story is a sad one, but don't be feeling too sorry for the town, for nowhere is it written that being busy and prosperous is necessarily an ideal. Where one city declines, another grows, and what is left behind is a town of different, though not necessarily worse, character. There's not much to do in Washington these days, but for those who like that sort of thing, it is a pleasant, quiet town, as opposed to the upstart railroad towns that surround it, which have themselves fallen victim to the highways. Washington can at least claim a grand past, dating to colonial times. It boasts of a few historic homes, a museum and a picturesque, cedar-lined cemetery. Those who come to explore that past can dine in two good restaurants including a cafe once called Enola's but renamed Prudhomme's. That's where the great chef's sister serves dishes that her brother made famous, at a better price, with none of the hassle and more of the hospitality. The town's restaurant industry at least prospers from the cooking tradition nurtured in St. Landry but popularized in New Orleans. Once more, Washington has a commercial link to the big city.

It also has a lesson to teach, and that is that sometimes cities, like people, are mourned for what they might have been, but with the passing of time they can be appreciated simply for what they were able to become.

Mother Of Mystics

It was a hot, truly muggy day in Mobile, Alabama, aggravated by the stench which a misdirected wind had carried into town from the nearby Scott paper plant. But at Oakleigh Plantation, just off the city's stately Government Street, one of the volunteer lady tour guides was unaffected by the smell. "In Mobile," she explained, "they say don't be concerned about the odor because it's the smell of money."

That juxtaposition of the plantation and the industrial pollution seemed to suggest something about the city, sometimes referred to as New Orleans' smaller sister city. Mobile is in a tug between its past and what is loosely described as "progress." The evidence is that progress is winning. Mobile has been casual about preserving its deep history. Although New Orleans and Mobile share a common ancestry (both cities were founded by Bienville), there is little in Mobile to suggest that French heritage, either in its buildings or its people. The town's best preservation is of the antebellum period, the period which most fits its character. In style and accent Mobile is a much more Southern city than New Orleans. And anyone who tries to experience its nightlife, or lack thereof, can tell that the cultural background of the city is more Southern Baptist than Latin. There is an advantage to that: Mobilians must certainly be better-rested people than New Orleanians.

Where progress has won its most solid victory is along the water-front, an area which could today be preserved as the old part of town, but which instead is the pathway for I-10's race between Pensacola and New Orleans. Historic old Fort Conde isn't even allowed its solitude; the Bankhead tunnel burrows beneath it.

There are remains of historic architecture, but most is overshadowed by uninspired modern design, the low-lights of which are a tubular Hilton that looks like it came from the chain's book of standard small-city hotel designs, and an auditorium made in the image of a miniature Superdome. There seems little evidence of public outcry for indigenous architecture in a city with a heritage for such.

Where Mobile and New Orleans do have a common bond is not in dome-like buildings, but in their carnivals. Mobilians like to point out that although New Orleans gets the publicity for its Mardi Gras, the Americanized tradition actually began in Mobile.

What actually happened was that a Mobilian, via Pennsylvania, named Michael Krafft, organized a New Year's parade in 1831, that became the forerunner of a carnival organization. In Mobile, the concept of mystic carnival organizations was created, and that concept was carried to New Orleans. Mobile is justified in calling itself the "Mother of Mystics".

It was Mobilians who were instrumental in creating New Orleans' first lasting carnival organization — the Mystick Krewe of Comus — back in 1857. So there is indeed a legacy from the Alabama city. What is generally overlooked, however, is that by the time of the Civil War, the Mobile Mardi Gras had died out. It wasn't until 1866, nine years after Comus began, that there was again a Mardi Gras celebration in Mobile. The Mobile parade borrowed from the New Orleans style and included New Orleans innovations such as tossing items from the floats. Mobile's top float builder from that period was from the Louisiana city.

Perhaps the proper metaphor for the relationship of the two cities and their carnival is that the seed came from Mobile but it was germinated in New Orleans, where it flowered, and from New Orleans cuttings were sent back to Mobile for planting. Each city contributed to the blooms.

Not that Mobile doesn't have enough blooms of its own. There are days — indeed most days — when the weather in the southern Alabama town is not hot and humid, and when the wind from the Scott plant is blowing away from town. On some of those days during the spring the azaleas are showing off their colors and Mobile is at its best. Signs for the Azalea Trail lead travelers through the swank parts of town, which are lush with purple-and pink-hued flowers. Mobilians boast, and rightfully so, of their azaleas and Mardi Gras, as well as the Senior Bowl football game and the Junior Miss beauty contest. It is a Southern town with mid-American values.

It is also a town with a promising economic future. Residents there talk about the "Tenn-Tom" with the same dollar sign fervor, although probably with more justification, that New Orleanians once showed towards the coming of the World's Fair in '84.

Tenn-Tom is the massive Tennessee-Tombigbee Waterway project, and Mobile will prosper as its Southernmost port. There's life downtown in anticipation of the renewed boom when Mobile can fully cash in on both the maladies and benefits of progress.

One day the Mother of Mystics might better be remembered as a daughter of commerce.

Smoky Row

A hundred years ago this week, Smoky Row was in its last days. Like the citizens of Pompeii, the residents of Smoky Row went about their lives perhaps realizing that there was a threatening force but uncertain when it would act.

In the case of Smoky Row, the force was the police who in July, 1885 yielded to public pressure and raided the one-block strip on Burgundy Street between Conti and Bienville streets. Its inhabitants were rounded up, some encouraged to leave town, and Smoky Row was no more. This was the sort of setting for which there would be neither nostalgia, nor mourning. The police, fearing the worst, looked for bodies in the patios and courtyards. There were none, but there were bloodstained wallets and piles of men's clothing. Such was life on Smoky Row.

Some of the vendors on the block became prominent within that dusty, steaming world. Among the more ornery were Gallus-Lu, Kidney Foot Jenny, Fightin' Mary and Sister Sal, the latter becoming known as One-Eyed Sal after a misunderstanding with Fightin' Mary. These ladies of commerce were fierce competitors.

That ferociousness clearly did not translate into charm. Male customers were sometimes drawn in not so much by sex appeal as by muscle. Stories claim that customers were sometimes literally dragged in off the streets; some were momentarily blinded by tobacco juice and robbed. Those were the lucky customers who were spared the pains of the baseball bats.

We still know about Smoky Row because of the commitment and genius of historian Al Rose who, in his classic book *Storyville, New Orleans* described the block's, "contentious inhabitants, numbering nearly a hundred female blacks who ranged in age from prepuberty to the seventies and engaged actively, one and all, in the game of commercial sex."

Imagine taking a Sunday afternoon stroll through the Quarter and spotting the gang along Smoky Row, lining the banquette with wicker rocking chairs while dipping snuff, chewing cigars and smoking pipes. According to Rose, the police and the press understandably saw these inhabitants as the most dangerous women in town.

And that was in a town where there was plenty of danger, such as on Gallatin Street on the river end of the Quarter, where residents included Red-Light Liz whose beau was Joe the Whipper. (Imagine their gift inscriptions at Christmas: To Red-Light from Whipper.)

The development of Storyville was part of the gradual effort to give more class and dignity to the practice of the oldest profession. But nowhere was prostitution practiced quite as it was along Smoky Row.

Today as the block faces its dubious centennial, it is about as passive a strip as can be found in the Quarter. Most of one side is now taken up by a sheet metal plant and part of the other side is the wall for a condominium development. In the evening the residents sit on their stoops, but it's for chatter with their neighbors. Few probably know the history of their block, but all can be grateful that, at least in this instance, the Quarter truly isn't what it used to be.

Frenchness

It was all so very French. As it happened, the evening that Frenchmen, led by Iberville, first slept on Louisiana soil was March 3, 1699. Someone might have looked at the calendar and noted that it was the day before Ash Wednesday, an observation which would leave writers to forever note that from the moment the French arrived here in the new world it was Mardi Gras.

If the French have a week that celebrates their national pride, it is the days before Bastille Day. In New Orleans, a town that celebrates the French Mardi Gras with far more fervor than do the Parisians, Bastille Day is one of the lesser ethnic celebrations. The feasts of the Italians and the Irish, two groups who arrived here much later than the French, are celebrated locally with much more vigor than the fall of the Bastille. Perhaps the reason is that the French were never an ethnic minority in New Orleans. In fact, they were the majority when the upstart Americans were a minority — so there's been less a sense of ethnicity among the descendents of the founders. Then, too, the term "French" has come to represent diverse people from Cajuns to Creoles(the latter term has shifted often through the years and is sometimes identified more with other nationalities). It says something of the French presence, though, that four of the city's last five mayors, two of whom were blacks, had French last names.

Through the years the visibility of the French presence locally has faded, although of late there has been a bit of a resurgence. There is now a French-operated and managed hotel on Canal Street, Le Meridien. French bakeries and croissant shops count among the most popular of the new restaurants in a town already saturated with eating places. The ultimate, however, happened when the Eiffel Tower restaurant opened on St. Charles Avenue. It is a grand boast for New Orleans' Frenchness that the restaurant that was once part of France's most famous landmark relocated right in the heart of what the Creoles use to dismiss as the "American sector."

It is a commercial victory that might have gladdered one particular French leader who was obsessed with wins and to whom, next to Lafayette, New Orleans probably owes the most, at least as a source for propaganda. Bienville founded the city but it was Napoleon who gave it prominence, by agreeing to sell the Louisiana territory. The move had great implications not only for national growth but for local tourism, which could point to the site where the nation's mid-section became part of the Union. Napoleon never came anywhere close to Louisiana, but his legend at least still sells wine at places like the Napoleon House.

In fact New Orleans is a Napoleon sort of town. We know of the emperor that he was not French by birth. The city's lineage is not entirely French either, but like the emperor it appreciates grandeur and has occasional pretense, even beyond its size.

Which leads to a theory of mine. In recent years there has been a fad over totebags with the description "Le Bag" written on the side. The bags have been a rage even among some who are clearly not French. My explanation for this is that secretly everyone really wants to be French, regardless of their nationality, just as New Orleans is a city that is American in fact but continues to be French in spirit.

Southern Comfort

Hattie Hardy should have moved. Her husband, the captain, was a railroad man who founded a settlement southwest of the Hardy's home in Meridian, Mississippi. But Hattie never had much use for her husband's settlement, not even when he named it after her. She preferred the bright lights and high living of Meridian instead, thus leaving the town of Hattiesburg to grow without the presence of its namesake.

If only Hattie had had a sense of history. This year Hattiesburg is celebrating its centennial, and the joke around town is that the folks are going to erect a statue of Hattie with an inscription at the base reading, "I'd rather be in Meridian."

That's about all the laughing that the southern Mississippi town is allowing about itself. Other than that, Hattiesburg, Mississippi is taking itself quite seriously as it enters its second hundred years.

Like most small towns, Hattiesburg's downtown streets are often deserted and many of the buildings are empty, but things are getting better. The old Saenger theatre on Front Street has been renovated and now houses live performances. The Memphis ballet is on the schedule and the New Orleans symphony is being courted.

Down the block, the old Forrest hotel is being restored into an office building complete with a rooftop restaurant. Across the street, City Hall has been rejuvenated, most of the rejuvenation taking place in the third floor office of Mayor Bobby Chain. In fact, Chain's office is one of the city's showpieces. It has been elegantly remodeled with solid wood paneling, plush sofas and chairs and elegant cabinets and desks. "The mayor believes that his office should show that we're serious here in Hattiesburg," one woman explained.

There is no question of misuse of funds in the restoration, since Chain financed his office renovation himself, as his gift to the city. In fact, doing things himself seems to be the mayor's style. The electrical contractor turned politician was once concerned that the homes in his block were getting run down. The solution: He bought and restored them, then sold them to friends who he knew would maintain them. The houses along the mayor's block all look very nice these days.

Chain recently converted to Republicanism and, as the story goes, the Mississippi Republican party sent him a congratulatory letter which included a check for $500 to be used in his next campaign. Chain sent the party a thank you note and returned the uncashed check along, with his own $500 contribution. They say that Chain has political ambitions beyond the Hattiesburg City Hall. No one knows for sure, but it may mean something that he keeps a jar of jelly beans on his desk.

His honor is not the only newsmaker in Hattiesburg during the centennial year. The home team, the University of Southern Mississippi, had a big season. USM is the largest university in the state, but because Ole Miss and Mississippi State have generally had better football teams, they are better known. This year was different. The Golden Eagles made it to a bowl game. Football season is over, but everywhere between Hattiesburg and the neighboring town of Laurel, the "Eagle Fever" signs are still on display.

Much of the town's economy depends on the lumber products industry but even though that industry has been in a slump there is prosperity in Hattiesburg. Huge stately new homes decorate the edges of town, with the largest, most stately and one of the newest going to the university president. Between Chain's office and the president's mansion, those who lead the town are at least able to do so in style.

Hattiesburg still suffers from small town dreariness. There are few restaurants and not much entertainment beyond that provided by the university. There are few natural attractions in the area and the zoo's couple of lions and its elephant can hardly maintain curiosity, or even interest, for very long.

Nevertheless, Hattiesburg on its 100th anniversary has a lot to be thankful for. There is leadership, energy and spirit. The town can also be thankful that Captain Hardy had the foresight to name the town after his prodigal wife and not after himself. Imagine if the signs on I-58 pointed in the direction of the cities of Laurel and Hardy. The town might never have been able to take itself seriously.

HOLIDAYS

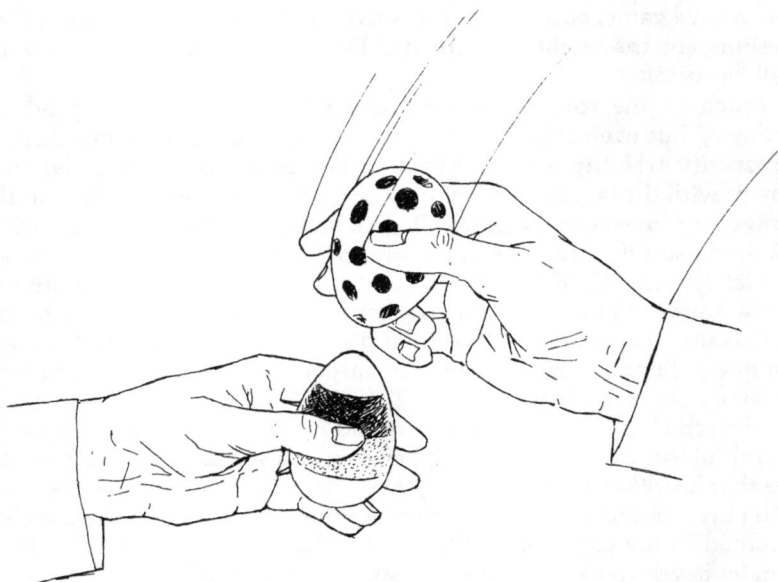

A True Custom

I'm worried about the St. Joseph's Day altars custom. There was a time when such altars were on display in many homes around town. The list in the Times-Picayune announcing when and where the altars could be seen was long and many New Orleanians made the trek to visit the displays.

Customs have a way of mellowing with time, of course. The St. Joseph's Day altar is endangered by changing lifestyles. There are fewer Italian mammas these days who have the time and inclination to spend hours in the kitchen making confections and baking fish, and their daughters are learning how to program computers rather than to stuff manicotti. But this is a custom that must be preserved, because it is unique to New Orleans. No Italians anywhere else outside of Sicily honor St. Joseph as he is remembered here. Even in New York's Little Italy, St. Joseph's Day is a minor event. (The attention there goes to St. Gennarro.)

It all began in the old country, when ancient Sicilians, as the story goes, prayed to St. Joseph to spare them from a famine. Once spared, they showed their gratitude by building altars made of food on the Saint's feast day — March 19. The custom came on the boat to New Orleans and stayed here. It is, more than the parades for St. Joseph or the Irish march for St. Patrick (both of which get more attention from the news media) a thoroughly local custom embellished by symbolism, faith, commitment and a pretty good hand in the kitchen.

Imagine the days when the Esplanade end of the Quarter was a vibrant Italian neighborhood and the doors of the little shotgun houses and Creole cottages opened to a front room dominated by a float-like altar filled with fig cakes, broiled fish, stuffed artichokes, fruits, Italian breads formed in the shape of crucifixes, and pastries made to look like an eye in honor of St. Lucia, a companion saint noted for her protection of sight.

As the local Italians moved so did the custom, to the dens and carports of new homes in Gentilly, Lakeview and Metairie. In one such setting I remember as a kid hearing an elderly Italian woman explain why she had labored on her altar. There had been a vision: one night she saw the figure of a saint, a visit which prompted her to annually build an altar.

Others have made the decision for reasons that are less dramatic — a tribute for a favor granted, quite often for an illness cured. In many homes, an elderly matriarch presides over the altar with the help of younger generations of daughters and sons who are the only hope that the custom will continue. It is a custom that involves more than just building an altar. There is, for instance, the ceremony on St. Joseph's Day still practiced at some homes where children dressed as Jesus, Mary and Joseph go through the ritual of knocking on different doors reciting their lines requesting entry. Not until the third try are they allowed in for the St. Joseph's feast.

Meat is never served, nor used in preparing the altar, narrowing the field of available edibles to just about everything else possible that could conceivably be served with pasta on the side. One food displayed though seldom eaten is the fava bean, which is blessed and given out as a good luck piece. (About three years ago there was a story in the local press about a grocer on the West Bank whose life was spared when a robber's bullet deflected off the "lucky bean" in his shirt pocket.) The fava bean was part of the crop that supposedly helped the ancient

Sicilians pull through their famine, thereby winning it special status centuries later in the New World, in a town where the folks would just as soon see beans served over rice with a link of sausage on the side.

That same town also enjoys Mardi Gras, another ritual rich in tradition and indigenous in character. Like our carnival, the altar custom has been expanded by Americanization and perhaps secularization. The huge public altars at the Italian Piazza and the St. Bernard Cultural Center are the Bacchus and Endymion of St. Joseph Day's — the grand spectacles which attract huge crowds.

Because of those altars the custom will no doubt survive over time in some form, at the very least as an historic curiosity and as a remembrance of the city's Italian heritage. But what is in danger are old line krewes of altardom, the displays in the homes overseen by grandmas and built from scratch with the help of doting daughters, sisters and neighbors.

Few customs can be as charming as people opening their homes to strangers to show off their artistry and share their belief. As times change, perhaps we may be heading towards a famine of such traditions. But then St. Joseph has been known to deal with famines before.

Egg Knocking

There are no egg knockers in the city. New Orleanians sometimes seem to think that they have a lock on local customs but there's only one that is popular in parts of the state, particularly in French Louisiana, that seems to have evaded the city. It's called egg knocking.

Egg knockers knock on Easter Sunday. The practice consists of gathering the stash of dyed boiled Easter eggs and then meeting the opposition. One person holds his egg firmly in hand, with the pointed end up. Another person takes an egg and with its pointed end taps the other. The tapping continues until an eggshell breaks. The losing egg goes to the winner. People with tough eggs are able to collect a whole salad full while making the rounds.

Sometimes this sport gets so infectious that people go for a second round with the already cracked eggs, this time using the rounded ends. It's kind of like playing the consolation game in a basketball tournament. Knocking with the round ends is okay, but it's the tough pointed-end competition that really counts.

As with most sports, a certain amount of folklore has evolved. One is the notion that if a person holds the egg firmly in hand while it is being knocked, the pressure will somehow spare it from being cracked. It doesn't work. Like an aging fighter, when an egg's time has come it comes, regardless of the gimmicks.

Another misconception is that dyed eggs taste better than regular boiled eggs. Some people will argue that with conviction. My theory is that dyed eggs do indeed taste different, if not better, than regular boiled eggs, but not because they are dyed. The real reason is that dyed eggs are usually boiled and colored a day or so before meeting their match on Easter. Thus the aging creates a fuller taste. Boiled eggs, on the other hand, are frequently eaten soon after being taken out of the pot. The taste is bound to be a bit different. Whatever the reason some seasoned knockers are determined enough to be successful in gathering eggs that occasional scams have developed.

One of the most common has been using the eggs of a guinea hen in place of those of a regular ole chicken. Guinea eggs are the brass knuckles of egg knocking. They are small and tough, and if there were a commissioner of egg knocking they would be illegal. A seasoned knocker knows to be aware of strangers with suspicious eggs.

Among those who compete fairly, fate can turn with each new opponent. Unlike most sports, prior records don't mean anything. An egg is only as good as its next challenge. Once it is cracked it retires, in defeat. The conquering egg is the new champ, but only until it loses its first match. This is one sport where there is no next season, no recovery time, no lingering glory.

Every Easter produces its good eggs — the ones that outlasted a half dozen or so before cracking up. Because the eggs are dyed different colors they develop distinct identities, sort of like jockey silks. But this is not a pastime for hero worship nor for sentiment. The people of French Louisiana have developed a hard-boiled attitude to egg knocking. As Easter Sunday passes the cheers cease, and one day's champ could be the next day's lunch.

Pumpkins

Halloween seems right for New Orleans — a city of old buildings and older legends with a heritage of voodoo queens and shallow graves. The day fits the city's character although there are some characters out there who do not befit the day. For the uninitiated, here are some tips for preparing one of the basics of Halloween — the jack-o-lantern:

Rule 1. Buy a drink at Molly's at the Market. Actually any other bar on or near Decatur Street will do as long as they get you near the French Market, which is where all respectable New Orleans jack-o-lanterns-to-be should be purchased. There are thousands of pumpkins to choose from, and the market, even in normal times, looks like Halloween should look. One group that is exempted from this rule is committed Yuppies (Young Urban Professionals), for whom the the schedule of films at the Prytania may not allow the time to go to the Quarter. They may purchase their pumpkins from the Whole Food Company. For purposes of making a jack-o-lantern it doesn't matter whether or not the pumpkins are organically grown.

Rule 2. Do not carve the pumpkin too early. A pumpkin is not like a Christmas tree. It can't stand around for a month. Once carved it begins to deteriorate and gets pretty messy after about 48 hours. Those who carve too early may indeed hear howling on Halloween night — from the neighbors who smell what remains of the pumpkin.

Rule 3. Don't get emotionally attached. No matter how cute the smiling face may be, be prepared to chuck it into the next day's garbage. There are some things in life that are not to be loved and a shriveled pumpkin is one of them.

Rule 4. Save the pumpkin meat. When scraping the inside save the fleshy part of the pumpkin, simply wrap it in foil and place it in the freezer so that it can be used in the future to make a pumpkin pie. Overlook for the moment the fact that no one you know likes pumpkin pie.

Rule 5. Buy long matches. Lighting the candle inside a jack-o-lantern is difficult since the match must extend vertically thereby causing the flame to burn up in the direction of the fingers. Lighting the candle outside the jack-o-lantern, then placing it inside, seldom works because the movement usually extinguishes the flame. Putting a flashlight or an electric bulb within is, of course, cheating. The best answer is a long match which allows time for the flame to contact the candle wick before reaching the fingers. Use of a butane torch is not considered appropriate.

Rule 6. Wait for the scorch smell. This is the best part. After the jack-o-lantern is first lit, wait a few minutes and then sniff the fragrance. The flame from the candle gradually heats the lining of pumpkin meat, causing an eventual caramelization. That accounts for the sweet, syrupy fragrance. That, of course, assumes the flame is not too large, in which case the smell might be of charred pumpkin, for which a fire extinguisher should be handy.

Rule 7. Remember the freezer. This takes place much later. Sometime around the following September remember to check your freezer and throw away the package of pumpkin scrapings from which a pie was never made.

There are pumpkins at the French Market this year that are so large that if they could be fired from a cannon, Gretna would be colored a splattered orange. They are so large that if they could float they could serve as blimps.

That may sound like pie in the sky, but the fact is that at the French Market the pumpkin crop is bountiful, featuring some that must have left the vine limp. Pumpkins, like people, seem to be getting bigger than ever.

There is no shortage of places for buying pumpkins but there's something about the French Market that just seems right. There's a harvest atmosphere there. The symphony of smell from the winter vegetables is that of the oncoming season. For city folk, the market is about as close as they can get to the farm and the farmers. Supermarkets are sterile and antiseptic. The market is genuine, peopled by those who camp out with their crop. A stray kitten finds a place for a cat nap between the protective shadows of two loose pumpkins.

A person might not know there can be so many varieties of pumpkins until he has surveyed the market. There are big round ones, some that are horizontal, others that are vertical. Most are a bright orange: some are pale.

At one stand the highest price was $15 for the biggest pumpkins, with prices descending according to size. One merchant, a Vietnamese woman, was indignant at the offer a customer had made for a small, softball-sized pumpkin. "No fifty cents," she answered, while poking a finger in the air so as to illustrate her price, 'One dollar." The customer seemed reluctant to double his offer.

The market has a life and character of its own, and although it is not a land of great wealth it is certainly a land of plenty. There is even, in this land, royalty. It is found at the entrance to the produce section of the market where a sign proclaims F & M Produce, the home of the "Garlic King."

It is fitting that on an island of vegetables, situated in a city of cooking, garlic should claim nobility. This domain is draped by dangling strands of garlic — there are huge garlic bulbs from California and smaller bulbs from Louisiana. But the King can read the calendar too. What distinguishes his stand, apart from the waves of dangling garlic strands, is his penchant for decoration.

Each year at harvest time the King, who apparently has learned the need for diversification, even among garlic specialists, decorates pumpkins — not by carving them, but by painting faces and even adding glitter. With the market as a backdrop there is quite a visual display, providing perhaps the world's only example of garlic and pumpkins mixing well. Top billing goes to the latter, however. Garlic, after all, may be king, but it's pumpkins that get to smile.

POLITICS

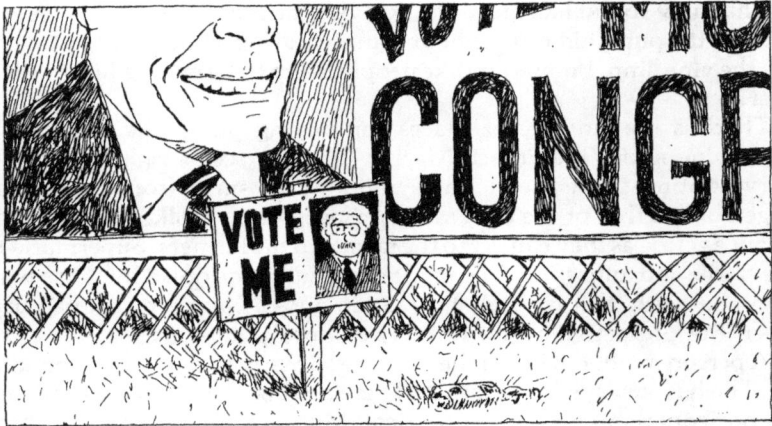

Learning Reality

Freddie has been learning a lot about democracy lately. It all began a few months ago, when he decided that he would run for the legislature. Sure, his opponents would likely be the incumbent and an attorney with lots of political connections, but Freddie was confident. No one he knew really liked the incumbent much, some people had never even heard of him; as for the attorney — well, everybody knew he was a wheeler-dealer who had gotten away with a zoning variance for his law office.

Freddie knew that once the campaign started and he could debate the issues with his opponents people would see that he was certainly the better candidate.

He was so enthusiastic about his candidacy that he started working before his opponents did. Those early days of the campaign were wonderful. All his friends assured him they were behind him, everyone he talked to pledged their vote and the lady next to the bank even agreed that Freddie could put a lawn sign in her yard. One day Freddie was driving around the district and the only signs of political activity he saw were his bumperstickers slapped on telephone poles. There was no sign of opposition; the race was beginning to look like a shoo-in. That evening Freddie even thought about running for Congress one day.

But then the mail came on the very day when Freddie was composing a letter to voters in his district. His mail included a full-color brochure with a picture of the lawyer and his friends, including someone who was supposed to help Freddie. The mailman also left a letter from the assessor urging his constituents to vote for the incumbent, reminding them how the legislator had fought against taxes.

Freddie dismissed all that as just politics, for he knew that the debate sponsored by a neighborhood group really make the difference. Once he could face the people, Freddie was confident he could turn the election his way. What Freddie hadn't counted on was that the people would not attend the debate, at least not people who were still undecided. The school cafeteria was packed that evening, but half of those there were wearing badges for the incumbent and the other half wore ribbons with the lawyer's name. The incumbent and the lawyer were booed and cheered by alternating halves of the crowd. When Freddie spoke, no one listened. A small item in the next morning's newspaper described the campaign as a race between the incumbent, the lawyer and a minor candidate. Freddie is still not sure just when his candidacy became minor.

But he still has hope. The candidate has given up on lawn signs and mailings and debates. Instead, he's counting on the people. He's sure that on election day the voters will see through the pomposity of the incumbent and the sleaziness of the lawyer and turn to Freddie.

What he's not counting on is the barrage of mailing for his opponents that will saturate the district in the closing week, nor the political endorsements for those two that will suddenly be announced. Neither is Freddie realizing that in the face of the onslaught by the opposition some of his friends will see him as a loser and vote for someone else. Freddie, and hundreds like him trying politics for the first time, aren't prepared for the hurt they will feel election night.

But in the end Freddie will profit because he will learn that his candidacy was minor because, while he did know something about government, he did not, in the end, know enough about politics.

Dutch On The Stump

His speech had reached the "Amen!" stage. Dutch Morial was on the stump, standing on a platform amidst a block party thrown to honor his bid for a third term. Looking down at the mostly black crowd that gathered along the 4000 block of Danneel Street, Morial spoke with a fervor that exemplified skilled political technique.

Speaking of his campaign, the mayor somehow drew interpretation of the city charter from the divine word. With each reference to an ancient passage the crowd responded with "Amens" and "Yeah you're right, brother." There was the spirit of a revival, only it was the city charter, rather than souls, that needed to be revived so that mayors could live on.

There were occasional hidden messages in the mayor's delivery, spoken to make a point to the home folk. Speaking of the effort in the 1960s to change the charter to allow then mayors extra terms, Morial explained that the voters rejected the idea, but then added, "and we all know who those voters were." The blacks in the audience nodded "Amen." They knew.

Reaching the home folk is part of the technique of such speeches, a technique that is well-established in Louisiana. If someone would have closed his eyes he could have imagined Earl Long preaching to his friends and neighbors in Winnfield — poor country folk who cherished the notion of having a governor for a friend.

Whatever point Uncle Earl was making, he probably used some of the same Bible references that Morial was using that day, and got the same responses. Earl had hidden messages, too, about the evils of an opponent from the big city. The crowd understood.

There were even similarities in dress. Morial wore suspenders that day, just like Uncle Earl, who would sometimes tug on them while he spoke. Political technique doesn't really change that much, just the audiences.

When Morial's speech was over, the band began with its own version of a campaign fight song. To the cry of "Who you're going to vote for?" the crowd answered, "Morial" — a response which didn't quite have the beat of "Ghostbusters," but no one seemed to mind, probably no more than any of the folks in Winnfield minded if Earl's fiddler was off-key. Politics makes its own music.

It also makes its own hope. This crowd was one that could have easily been alienated by politics, but on this afternoon its members were feeling like part of the in-crowd that they were. Like the folks in Winnfield applauding Earl or the Irish saluting the Comiskeys and the Burkes, the people were mixing with one of their own who had achieved power. Vicariously they shared that power, and perhaps felt a bit better about themselves.

After some announcements about free hot dogs and beer and an upcoming barbecue, followed by a group singing "Happy Birthday" to Civil Sheriff Paul Valteau, the mayor worked his way through the crowd. He is a bright, savvy executive who can be just as skilled and equally conversant shaking hands at the National Conference of Mayors as on Danneel Street.

There are some who would look down on the rally as politics at its worst. But if a people whose parents were seldom able to even get near a mayor felt that day more like a part of the community, it may have really been democracy at its best.

Reign's End

Sometimes when dynasties fall it's not with a thunder but with a whisper. That's the way it was in May, 1985, when 51 years of control of the First Municipal District assessor's office by the Comiskey family ended. Different challengers have been wanting to oust the family for years, but when the end came it was quiet, and even predictable.

There have been changes in other assessors' offices this year but none were as historically significant as the end of the Comiskey regime because no political family name continued for so long, and no family had such a lasting hold over a section of town.

It is a family name that evokes nostalgia from old-time ward politics. Jim Comiskey was one of the new breed of Irish politicians who a half-century ago were, like blacks today, finding politics to be a quick and reachable route to assimilation. And assimilate he did, becoming the boss of the Third Ward. Legends abound about the weekly meetings at Comiskey headquarters where constituents would bring their problems to the boss, whose repetoire included just about any public service not just something as mundane as keeping property taxes low. Sidewalks were repaired and services rendered from what became an adjunct City Hall.

But those who received owed, and those who opposed had to fight. One man I know recalls the morning in 1946 when he was working for the upstart DeLesseps Morrison in his attempt to unseat Bob Maestri from the mayor's job. Comiskey was backing the incumbent, so the Third Ward was Maestri territory. The man was assigned by the Morrison camp to be a poll commissioner in the Comiskey home precinct. He dutifully arrived at the poll at 5:45 that morning, 15 minutes ahead of the announced time for his swearing-in as commissioner. Only that proved to be too late; a slate of Comiskey commisioners had been sworn in at 5:30. Such was politics in the dynasty.

But the truth is, the term "dynasty," when applied to the last decade, is an overstatement. As politics changed, what remained was less a dynasty than a family tradition. Jim was replaced by his nephew, Lawrence, who served during a period when outside influences were gradually diminishing the political strength of assessors. One new influence was the emergence of the black vote, which responded to a different set of political bosses. Then there was the emerging neighborhood movement, which created new leaders who were quite capable of dealing with City Hall on their own. Changes in the assessment system made arbitrary evaluations less likely. Finally, there was the overall decline of machine politics, meaning there were fewer privileges to give away, fewer strings to pull.

Still, somebody had to be assessor, and the voters were content to let it be Jim's nephew. There are those in political life who have strong and occasionally bitter feelings about other politicians, paricularly rivals, but I prefer to remember Larry Comiskey outside of the electoral setting as a nice guy.

I last saw him during the Carnival season of 1984. He was dressed in formal wear as he watched the Babylon parade pass in front of Gallier Hall. Having spotted me, a constituent, across the street, he motioned to one of the ushers to make a delivery. The usher arrived with a handful of doubloons. Comiskey waved and grinned from across the way. It was old fashioned assessorial politics at its most innocent — give 'em doubloons and keep the taxes low.

From the moment Connie Comiskey took over her father's unexpired term, she had to be running. There would be an election and the opposition would be strong. Political realities being what they are, there would have been nowhere else for her to go politically. Had the majority allowed it she would probably have spent her professional career as assessor, doing a competent job of it.

In the last days of the Comiskey reign, the power base was long gone but there still was an emotional hold. To many of the old families in Mid-City, Connie Comiskey was the continuation of what they had always had with government. Councilmen, mayors and bureaucrats changed, but there were always the Comiskeys to lend stability. Providing the people with a sense of closeness and confidence in government is not a bad service, and the old-line assessors did just that.

Now there will be a new assessor whose political evolution, like that of the Comiskeys, was on the strength of ethnic politics. There will be a new circle of people who feel better about government because the assessor is their neighbor.

Less than an upheaval, it's a natural development, because in democracy public office is ultimately won and not inherited.

Transitions

My first impression of the mayors of New Orleans was a horse. Each year the police unit in the Carnival parades would be led by a mounted officer whose steed wore a blanket with the name "Chep" on the side. Old Chep turned out to have a lasting name because deLesseps "Chep" Morrison's tenure in City Hall lasted nearly 16 years. The entire baby boom generation went from infancy to puberty knowing only one mayor.

Then one Carnival, the same policeman was riding a different horse, this one named Vic. Vic lasted for a decade before being replaced by Moon. The equestrian tradition somehow stopped during the Landrieu years, thereby depriving the city of ever seeing a horse named Dutch trot by. The custom's end is just as well, mercifully sparing some animal from being known as Sidney.

Mayors, it seems, have been more important in New Orleans than they might be in other cities. One reason might be that there have been so few of them. Since 1946, there have been only four: Chep Morrison, Vic Schiro, Moon Landrieu and Dutch Morial. With such infrequent change at City Hall, it has been easy to mark time by administrations.

Perhaps more than half the city grew up during the Morrison years. In this, the week before the inauguration of a new mayor, the mind wanders to past transitions. In a John Chase cartoon in the old New Orleans *States*, two teenagers are looking at a headline announcing that Morrison had resigned his position to become an ambassador. One kid tells the other he didn't know it was possible for the city to have another mayor.

A few years later, Morrison was the center of an urban trauma. News came of an airplane crash in Mexico. A generation learned about life's hard realities as it filed past Morrison's casket at Gallier Hall.

Vic Schiro's years are starting to look better in retrospect. At the time, a playful generation recognized only a playful mayor donning his fatigues during a hurricane or mastering the art of ribbon cutting. People laughed. Years later, from the perspective of a recession, one could only wish there were more ribbons to be cut.

Both the generation and the city seemed to reach full maturity during the Landrieu years. Integration was no longer an issue, it was a mandate. A domed stadium was completed. The mayor became a national spokesman for cities. It all seemed so grown-up.

Dutch Morial came into office with fanfare and a bash at Lafayette Square. Two days after his inauguration, some activists set up solar screens on the front lawn of City Hall to celebrate Sun Day — a tribute to the wonders and potential of solar energy. They couldn't have picked a worse day. The rains came, touching off the worst internal flooding in the city's modern history. A stormy stewardship in the mayor's office had begun.

Eight months later, Morial was facing a walkout by the police during Mardi Gras. A reporter told me of having been in the governor's mansion one afternoon when Edwin Edwards, who was in his second term, received a call from the mayor and teased, "Dutch, what's wrong down there? Since you've been mayor, all we've had is floods and strikes."

Those situations, however, were when Morial was at his best — an intensely intelligent, strong-willed person standing steadily at the helm.

It is too soon to judge his performance objectively. There are also some wounds to be healed, though the fact that wounds have become part of the conversation may contribute to that assessment. I prefer to remember him as a tough guy doing a tough job. And among politicians there is a certain respect for toughness: Both Edwards and Morial were once at a campaign rally at the Fairmont. Morial gave a brief speech in which he made a joking reference to perhaps going upstairs later and shooting some craps with the governor. Edwards followed with his own preamble that, "I may not be the smartest person in the world, but I have enough sense not to shoot craps with a black politician."

Morial, too, could mark time by mayoral terms. He once told me of the first time he saw a mayor — as a boy when Robert Maestri visited a schoolyard. That visit may have not only inspired Morial but the city's future as well.

Mayors come and go, but inspiration lingers: now there will be a new mayor and a new time frame. A new generation will be introduced to politics. And there will be new stories to be told. And perhaps, for some particular school child, a lasting memory to be made.

ℝAILS

500 Miles Before Dawn

It's dark outside as the Crescent rumbles through North Carolina. As seen from the window of the roomette, the occasional house and street lamps spark the way along the passing landscape. There's something almost hypnotic about staring at the countryside from the window of a train. A cassette of train songs loaned by a friend adds to the effect. At this moment, the selection is a John Prine generation folk tune entitled, "No One Cares About The Railroads Anymore."

That some people still do care keeps Amtrak's Crescent in business. Each morning it leaves New Orleans and begins its trek to the east. It wiggles past the backyards of Gentilly, then teeters along the levee past the Little Woods fishing camps. Next the train enters one of the most incredible pieces of track in all railroading — the run over Lake Pontchartrain via the Rigolets trestle. The feeling is one of being in a linear boat, surrounded by water, speeding towards a distant port. Fishing boats are alongside, right outside the window — as though they are part of the fleet.

Soon the Crescent rushes across the Mississippi state line and the kudzu belt. From Picayune to Atlanta the scenery is lush with the green vine that conquered the South. As the train rushes through the woods, the kudzu which has draped stumps, trees and miscellaneous inanimate objects creates formations which are sometimes bizarre. The forest is filled with green silhouettes of strange things.

Many passengers no doubt miss the sights because they are preoccupied with eating. Food consumption has always been a notable pastime on the Crescent, dating back to the days when Southern Railway operated the train. Then it was noted for its dining car, in which the food was cooked on board in an oven heated with wood. Nothing could be finer than to be in Southern's diner in the morning, speeding across the lake while chomping into a slice of ham. Because the Southern Crescent was the very last long distance train to be operated by private enterprise, rather than Amtrak, it was a natural for publicity. Many writers related their experiences of riding the South's finest train.

But time and the economy forced even Southern to give up its train, and now Amtrak is at the throttle. Things have changed. There's still a dining car but the grill is gone. Rather lethargic waiters serve the prepared dishes heated in a convection oven. The food actually isn't bad, but to anyone with memories it's not the same. The cars in the train are rather plain, owing mostly to the several tunnels along the route which prohibit Amtrak from using its shiny new double-deck coaches. The fact is that although the Crescent has gotten good press through the years, it isn't even the best train to run out of New Orleans. The best is the Sunset Limited, the all double-decker train that rambles to Los Angeles three times a week.

Still, the Crescent is a good and efficient train. It leaves New Orleans early one morning and arrives in Washington on the next morning, seldom late. There are some compulsive people in this world who time the train in which they are riding, double-checking to see if it reaches each stop on time. Count me in; the Crescent was right on time at every stop both coming and going.

Clock watching, however, is almost inconsistent with the spirit of train riding. You can't be in a hurry to ride a train. Using sports as a comparison, I have a theory that people who like trains are also likely to prefer baseball, while football fans prefer to fly. The difference is an appreciation for passivity and exploration over speed, the frantic need to get somewhere in a hurry. Refueling in Birmingham is the equivalent of changing pitchers — it is a break in the action. While some people would get tense over the inactivity, baseball fans and train riders would see such a break as merely an opportunity for a good stretch.

Train prices are competitive only if a passenger is riding coach. Rooms are expensive, far more so than taking a plane. Trains, over a long distance, can't be justified financially. In fact, the only real justification, except for those who fear flying, is that trains let you see the land and villages that bridge the destinations. The great American in-between passes by.

Consider, for example, the first hours of daylight as the Crescent streaks through Virginia. The signs point to places like Manassas and Charlottesville. The land is hilly. The people in the small-towns are leaving for Sunday morning services. A touch of the button on the cassette recorder and Arlo Guthrie is singing, "Good Morning America, How are you. . . " Did you ever wonder why they never write songs about airplanes?

Making Tracks

His hopes had been dashed. A local teacher had had a great idea for his costume for the parade marking the sesquicentennial of the St. Charles streetcar. He had called Maison Blanche department store and arranged to borrow the store's Mr. Bingle costume. At first it had **seemed like the store would go along with the request, but at the last** minute the idea fell victim to corporate-think and refusal.

In retrospect, the refusal may have been just as well, for it is written that there is no higher position that a mortal can obtain than to ride in a New Orleans streetcar while dressed as Mr. Bingle. After that there is nothing else to look forward to.

With the burden of the honor denied him, the man could at least look forward to the party to follow at the Willow Street car barn. The barn is the home and hospital for the aged trolleys. It is a place where men have labored on and loved the electric vehicles, and on that day the love seemed to have finally been answered.

As the story goes, a senior foreman at the car barn, a man who has spent 40 years working on streetcars and whose father and grandfather once operated the vehicles, looked around with astonishment at the crowd that had come to the home of the streetcar on its birthday. The man had been around for the bad old days. He had been part of the work crew that had dismantled some of the Canal Street streetcars when the line was discontinued. He had heard the rumors about the trolley sevice being phased out completely. But on this day, as the streetcars were getting more attention than he had ever seen, he felt the emotion and began to cry. No one could blame him. Parenthood had been rewarded. There will never be such sentiment for a city bus.

Sentiment, as it was, was spread along the tracks. At least once each hour the Cable News Network was telling the nation about this strange celebration in New Orleans, a celebration where those who wanted to could ride the trolleys for free and get off at will to experience pockets of entertainment. The pockets were fullest at Audubon Park, where the packed streetcars rolled past a tent and a bandstand, each filled with music. There were the accoutrements of such festivity, such as inflatable beer bottle balloons and the table from which the inevitable commemorative posters were sold. There was also lots of space for spreading blankets from which to marvel at the blue sky and feel the October breeze. The clang of the streetcar only added to the mood.

Plenty more clanging was to be done, especially that evening when nearly 30 of the streetcars, decorated with balloons, lined alongside Lafayette Square for a streetcar parade. The passenger list included some dressed in early century costumes as chimney sweeps, Christmas presents, and members of a barbershop chorus. Many rode dressed simply as themselves. Some tried to make themselves even more apparent, notably the politicians tracking along the trolleys, looking for hands to shake and chests to display their badges.

Most conspicuous among the streetcars was the line's one early-century model — the antique Ford, Davis, Bacon trolley that can sometimes be spotted along the track serving as a repair vehicle. This day its assignment was more joyous, as it carried the New Reliance Jazz Band. But then, music can sometimes repair the spirit.

At what was more or less the announced time the parade began to roll. The streetcars marched in clumps of ten so that the power from above would not be overworked. Along the route a curious public, one that is well conditioned to parades, sat and watched one of the more unusual parades to ply the Avenue, a parade with floats of green that marched to the beat of a clang.

As it wound along St. Charles, the procession was spotlighted by the first evening of the harvest moon, the fullest, brightest moon of the year. It was fully appropriate because, on this rare night in New Orleans, if appreciation were a crop, the harvest would have been bountiful.

WEATHER

Summer Solace

Down here in the semi-tropics where the sun steams the air, it was Congress rather than astronomers that showed more insight. According to thesolar charts, summer doesn't begin until June, but then Congress created Memorial Day — a holiday which came to signal the beginning of summer, perhaps a bit too early in Yankee tundra, but already a tad late along the Southern rim, where the azalea's springtime gift of color is faded and forgotten in pursuit of the golden rain tree's patch of shade.

Summer is enemy to New Orleans, the clash having created such evacuation centers as pine-cooled Abita Springs, shoreside Biloxi and Gulfport. In the years before Fedders and friends would cool homes while emptying streets, the best New Orleans summer pastime was simply to leave.

Those who stayed were offered sparse recreation. There were evenings at Pontchartrain Beach amusement park, where the Zephyr made its own breeze. And there was fishing along the seawall. Cold watermelon for a hot night was a popular roadside item, until the air conditioner made it more inviting to just stay inside.

In return for its few pleasures, summer counters with welt-sized discomforts. Beyond the heat and humidity there is the mosquito, an attack jet with the propulsion to penetrate the heavy air. Worse yet, there's the mosquito fogger, a rackety vehicle that seems to hold its fire of fly poison spray until the doors and windows of homes along its route have been opened in hope of fresh air. This is the mosquitoes' playful revenge, its lark being worse than its bite.

The weather is monotonous: hot mornings, rainy afternoons, then muggy evenings. Towards summer's end, the monotony is broken occasionally, but by hurricanes. The last mile of the trip from Memorial Day to Labor day is driven through tropical winds. The hurricanes rule the day — the eyes have it.

Through its suffering, however, New Orleans has somehow managed to make a pair of contributions to the way America spends summer — both as defenses from the weather. One was the rain check, a concept created by Abner Powell, whose hapless New Orleans Pelicans baseball team was beleaguered by rainouts more than strikeouts. The other was the Ortolano Sno-Wizard machine, perhaps not the first machine to change ice into edible snow but the first and finest of such machines to be mass produced, creating a snow far superior to the hopeless ice-crushing machines used at alien county fairs. The rectagular-shaped Ortolano machine made possible a local snowball industrial complex. In the war against summer, snowballs became the city's only lasting weapons.

Most simple summer pleasures, however, have for the most part been denied New Orleanians, people who live in a city where a dip in the lake is preceded by an inquiry, not about the temperature but the bacteria count. The age of the air-conditioned convention hall has allowed for new events, such as the Food Fest, to claim a spot on the sparse summer calendar; and organizers of La Fete, a summer festival, have learned that what works best is that which is held inside, particularly inside restaurants, where the food can be hot, as long as the location isn't.

Given the odds against it, New Orleans has done about as well as can be expected against the summer. If the city had a baseball team it would no longer need the rain check — because the locals would play in an air-conditioned stadium with a dome on top. And mosquito control programs have sized down the fleet of the critters. But there will always be nights when the sky seems to jump from heat lightning and when the banana leaf's sway provides the only breeze. Man and his inventions have put up a fight, but in the end summer always wins.

Rain

Rain has a way of setting a mood, especially in New Orleans where it is so much a part of the character of the city. Rain slides off steep roofs, glides along gutter paths then swirls down spouts, creating that gurgling sound that is part of the rhythm of the semi-tropics. Last Saturday night, I stood on an uptown porch watching the rain driven by the wind of a tropical storm pelt a banana tree. The leaves seemed to stagger from the pounding. Tropical storm, rain, banana trees. In an old town rich with images there is a special romance to rain.

There is also a struggle against it. New Orleans has a curious relationship to water. In terms of flood protection, this town was built where a city should not have been built. But the Mississippi River was diverted from its course (through the area just outside New Orleans) by a chain of spillways. The site also is naturally below sea level, which means that the city could not drain naturally, so an urban miracle, a system of pumps was created.

In recent years, however, the water has taken its revenge against its conquerers. Although the river no longer causes floods, the rain does, because the ancient pumping stations cannot keep up with the city's growth. The high waters that earlier planners had sought to eliminate come, not from the other side of the levee but from the dark side of the skies. The rain even flooded the streets while defying voters to increase the funding for city drainage. Rather than pay for improvements the voters resisted the dare. After all, a little high water now and then is good for the spirit, if not for the living room floor.

Sometimes, however, the rain can make the spirits soggy, which is why New Orleans' most famous contribution to sports is the rain check — the New Orleans Pelicans baseball team's answer to games that were rained out in progress. Dripping fans at least knew that their ticket stubs would gain them entry to another game, perhaps one when the night was clear, or perhaps on a night infested by mosquitoes, the night raiders of the rain, who use puddles as their runways.

naturally, has been blamed for the increase in flooding. (Caused, of course, by heavy rains). There's no denying the elements in the semi-tropics.

Nor should they be denied. Weather-watching is a serious pastime in this city, where meteorologists figure among the local TV stars. For most of the year the forecasters routinely tell the citizens to expect scattered afternoon thundershowers. It is a prediction that is not only, well, predictable, but fortuitious as well, because New Orleans never looks better than it does right after a rain.

Uptown, along Canal Street, and especially in the Quarter, there's something special about the first few minutes after a rainfall, as though this eccentric Latin city has undergone a cleansing ritual. The wheels from the horse-drawn buggies swish in the rain, the horse's clomp splashes in the puddles. The balconies reflect from the street. The air is clean, all the better to clear the way for the scents from the newly scrubbed foliage. This is the stuff of artists' sketch pads.

There is suddenly the vitality of rebirth. A city shamed by its litter seems cleansed. A city known for its sluggishness had found energy. New Orleans reveals itself as a city cast by the river but designed by the rain. It is, after all, a town that nature, in the great scheme of things, must surely have saved for a rainy day.

Nash

Some of the old-timers in the Rex organization tell the story about the time when rain seemed to be threatening the carnival day parade. While krewe members paced in their den, Rex's lieutenants and captains consulted Nash Roberts, who, in addition to his reputation as the city's premiere television weatherman, was also lesser-known as His Majesty's Royal Meteorologist.

Roberts consulted his charts and maps and then advised the captain that if the parade's lead unit left at a given moment the procession would escape the rain. On cue, the captain ordered the parade to roll. Rex led the way along his route, reveling in a rainless reign. The skies, as though directed by Roberts, were civil while the parade rolled, holding back until the precise moment when the last float entered the unloading area at the end of the route. A downpour began, but Roberts' calculations had kept Rex dry.

A local television news anchor once complained of the volatile nature of the TV news business; one moment you're in, then you're out — and hurt. But that wasn't going to happen to him, he told me, because he had a model. "Look at Nash Roberts," he said, "he has his own business and his own security outside of TV. If he had to leave television tomorrow, it wouldn't hurt him one bit."

As of last week, Nash Roberts has indeed left television (by his choice) and, judging by his jovial mood as he made his farewell on WWL-TV's evening newscasts, he seemed less hurt than relieved. No one in local or network television history — not even such fixtures as Captain Kangaroo, who holds the network longevity record — has been on television longer than Roberts, who spans three decades and three different stations.

When the history of New Orleans during the last half of this century is written, mention will have to be made of Roberts, who was more visible to a larger audience than perhaps any figure in the city's history. Mayors, actresses, generals, voodoo women — no one in the city's character-filled past has played a bigger house, and when hurricanes were on the way, no one ever commanded more of this city's attention.

Roberts will probably be best remembered for those long nights in the studio as storms named Audrey, Betsy and Camille headed our way. What most New Orleanians who have lived in this town more than a decade know about hurricanes, they probably learned from Roberts.

I will remember him also for the hundreds of times he stood before the television camera routinely reciting the standard New Orleans weather prediction — "partially cloudy and mild with a chance of scattered afternoon thundershowers." I'll remember him from the early days of television when sports sidekick Mel Leavitt would introduce the weather segment by asking, "Hey, Nash, what's the scoop on the weather?" More often than not the scoop was, "partially cloudy and mild.."

I will remember him for the time when it did rain on Mardi Gras (probably before Rex made him meteorologist) and the weathercast opened with a close-up shot of Roberts with a noose around his neck. And I remember the time the city was covered with white and Roberts had to hand scrawl a sign that said "snow" in place of the prepared placards that were routinely used to announce "rain' or merely "cold."

But more than all those things, there is something else for which he should be appreciated — after all, while he was a good weatherman, his predictions were seldom any different from his competitors' and his broadcasts were frequently less gripping. What distinguished Roberts was his survivability. A Nash Roberts could never make it in television today — having neither the clinical good looks nor the polished tones of the modern broadcaster. Yet Roberts not only survived but wrote his own ticket along the way. A natural victim for the ratings war, Roberts instead benefitted from it. His leaving Channel 6 for Channel 8 was greeted with much ballyhoo. Broadcasters stumbled over each other to project a local image, thus making it natural that Channel 4 would trumpet even greater fanfare when it lured Roberts away from Channel 8. Had Nash Roberts never left Channel 6, his parting from television might have been long ago, but instead, each station change bolstered his reputation. In an industry sorely in need of one, Roberts was a local guy who knew what he was talking about.

No other weatherman (or meteorologist, as they have come to be known) could insist that his 10 p.m. news segments be taped earlier in the evening (with the possibility of his coming in live if the weather changed). No other weatherman could at various times have his brother and a son working different weather shifts on television. In an industry where faded stars suddenly disappear, without the chance to say goodbye, few weathermen could end their career amidst applause, tears and a present — a weather vane for his farm.

And that is what distinguished the television career of Nash Roberts. He was a nice guy, a regular guy who, instead of being crushed by television, somehow managed to conquer it.

WORLD'S FAIR

The Night Of The Bag People

It was nine o'clock on a Saturday evening at the World's Fair. A comedian on stage at Jed's Lookout was displaying an official World's Fair plastic rain parka as though it were a piece of high fashion. He joked that he didn't see anybody wearing them anymore, although they had been popular as recently as earlier that week. It just shows how trendy people can be about fashion," he added. The weather for the past two days had been hot and dry.

At 9:30 that evening, some of the last of the evening's visitors filed through the Historic New Orleans Collection's Rain" exhibit. There they learned that the fair's host city is annually saturated by downpours. Further saturation, however, seemed unlikely that evening.

By 10:30, everyone's attention shifted to the riverfront, where skyrockets were flaring into the clear night sky. Two hours later, Fulton Street and the Italian Village would be packed with people enjoying the good weather and the night life.

At 1:30, the weather began to change rapidly. the wind became stronger and the air more moist. "We'll have to pause to change a string on this guitar," the band leader on the Italian Village's stage announced. The break was just as well, because the band had lost its audience, which was hurrying for cover as the rain intensified.

There are many stories to tell about the fair in New Orleans, and one of them is about the evening a sudden storm hit the fair site afterhours. Most of the fair buildings were closed by then, including the Convention Center, so the storm forced clusters of people to huddle beneath overhangs, monorail ramps and the recesses of buildings. The sky was white with summer lightning.

By 2:15, the storm had reached its full rage, sending water sprays ricocheting along Front Street, creating a wonderfall. Streams raced down the fair walkway, heading straight to the mouth at the opening of a drain. The lights of the water garden were made hazy by the sheets of falling water.

Meanwhile, the refugees endured, distracted from their soggy agonies by the likes of fellow travellers splashing and performing in the streets. A thousand or so people caught in a storm were having an adventure.

By 2:30, there was a new addition to the waterlogged pageantry — groups of garbage bags, some holding hands, were marching by. The bags had becomes hot items because of their adaptability as makeshift parkas. At Pasta Vincenzio, dripping customers stood in line to pay 25 cents apiece for trash bags which could be pulled over their heads. A small hole would be torn through in the vicinity of the nose.

Suddenly, it was the night of the bag people — strange creatures consisting of bag-shaped bodies and pairs of legs. They roamed the fair site and its vicinity in clusters, looking like tribes of overgrown beignets in search of warm coffee. The chatter in the streets included bag people humor — feigned fear of being picked up by the garbage men, and whimsical suggestions of checking into one of the nearby posh hotels and telling the doorman, "These are my bags."

But such humor would not have life beyond 3:00 that morning, when the rain stopped. The moving clouds unveiled a clear sky. Plastic garments were discarded. The bag people were no more. Once again during that night in the semitropics further rain seemed unlikely.

The Last Hour

It was quite a scene — Lindy Boggs, Seymour D. Fair and Irma Thomas swaying arm in arm on the stage of the amphitheatre, singing "Auld Lang Syne" in unison. Around them stood a hundred or so other people all joining in as the fair reached its last moments. Then suddenly the stage's backdrop opened, revealing the river, from which bright flares were fired providing a curtain of sparking red and yellow. The popping sound and the applause from the stands were overcome by Thomas, who by then had moved towards the band and on cue began singing Lionel Ritchie's "All Night Long," just as Ritchie himself had done for the closing of the Olympics. Those on stage shuffled to the melody but the mood was mixed — the music suggested party, but the party was over.

Few events mixed moods as did our World's Fair, the Cuisinart of expositions. Even in the final moments, fairgoers' moods were well mixed. Some were disappointed over the financial problems and bad publicity, others appreciative of the Fair itself. Thus it was consistent that Fair president Petr Spurney, booed by a few as he reached the podium to declare the fair closed, was then mobbed by people seeking his autograph. In the final hour, what was good about the fair was being felt.

Spurney signed while the river to his left was set ablaze with the fair's last fireworks display. The rockets flowered the sky with blinking haze, providing enough illumination to quickly silhouette the ships sliding along the river. From those ships came loud whistles, which somehow seemed in harmony with the thunder from the fireworks and the reverberation of Thomas' song. There was light, color and music — all penetrating the crisp November air. It was reminiscent of that hot day in May when the fair opened to the accompaniment of birds, balloons and blimps. People eyeing the gondola, the monorail and the Wonderwall for the first time spoke of the "sensory overload" of it all. The overload wasn't as burdensome in the dark of November but the emotion was still heavy.

There was also a tinge of emotion at the Italian Village, where the Circus DiCarlo went through the paces of its last performance at the fair. The next stop, Chalmette, would not be as glamorous as a world exposition but the show must go on. As the crowd filed from the little big top DiCarlo himself delivered his standard closing announcement — "remember someday, somehow, the Circus DiCarlo may be in your town."

For the fair's biggest star the prospects were more glorious —

Washington D.C. and immortality. During the closing ceremonies Seymour D. Fair, the ham that this pelican was, slid down a rope to accept a medal commemorating his acceptance by the Smithsonian Institute as a permanent exhibit. The fair had its faults but it produced a great animated cheerleader costume. No display will ever capture Seymour's humor nor reveal the secret that I learned. Early in the fair, I was sitting on a bench near Centennial Plaza when Seymour happened to walk by. He stopped, turned to me, touched the baseball cap I was wearing and raised his hands in a symbol of victory. Seymour, it turns out, was a Boston Red Sox fan. The Sox and the fair both had disappointing seasons, but their boosters persisted.

Seymour wasn't around by ten that evening, when the last visitors were herded away. All that was left were a few hundred people attending a private party in front of the U.S.A. pavilion. There was a band and plenty to eat and drink but the mood was a bit somber. In the distance, the glow of the fair grounds was shining for the last time. For years there had been anticipation, then the actual experience. Now the lights were going out. Someday, somehow, the circus would be in another town, but for New Orleans it was over.

WOULD-BE LEGENDS

New Orleans needs some fresh legends. The old legends — the ones that are not true — are running thin. For a new generation of tourists we need to do more than just get them to believe that Canal Street was built on a canal or that Napoleon slept at the Napoleon House. Just as retailers increase their stock for the tourist invasions, we need to increase our supply of historical untruths. To wit:

• Haagen-Dazs ice cream parlor in the Quarter was founded by two Swedish sailors, Hans Haagen and Fritz Dazs, who jumped ship in New Orleans. Coincidentally, the term "Haagen Dazs" in Swedish means, "Give me two scoops of rum raisin and hold the onions."

• Jackson Square was named after entertainer Michael Jackson. The statue in the middle of the Square is of a horse standing on its hind legs trying to do Jackson's famous backwards shuffle-step. The horse's rider is doffing his hat as a symbolic salute to "Thriller" as the number-one-selling LP of all time.

• In the early days of the city, Choctaw Indians hunted for nutria on the strip of land that runs down the middle of Canal Street. The Choctaws referred to the land as their "nutria ground," a term which the European settlers mispronounced as "neutral ground."

• Jazz was invented on WSMB radio during the Nut and Jeff show one morning when a 45 rpm blues recording was mistakenly played at 78 rpm. The speeded-up sound was such a hit that callers kept the lines busy asking for more. Both Nut and Jeff agreed that the lively tempo of the new music reminded them of a well-executed fast break in basketball, hence they named the new sound after the city's then-pro basketball team — the New Orleans Jazz.

• New Orleans is known as the Crescent City because of its citizens' fondness for croissants — crescent rolls — served with their meals. The introduction of croissants to local kitchens was considered to be a big improvement from the days when the town was known instead as the Melba Toast City.

• Anyone who catches 30 gold-colored doubloons in the parades of Momus, Proteus, Comus or Rex may bring them to Antoine's Restaurant and cash them in for a free four-piece pompano dinner to go, complete with cole slaw and a biscuit. With an additional 10 silver-colored doubloons from the same parades, recipients will be awarded a side order of souffle potatoes and a large Big Shot Cola.

• During World War II a Nazi submarine entered Lake Pontchartrain. Its mission was cut short, however, when it happened to float headlong into the flow of debris from the Jefferson Parish sewerage system. The crew surfaced and surrendered but was released under the Geneva Convention prohibition against chemical warfare.

• The Irish Channel was named after a television station that once broadcast from the corner of Constance and Third streets, at the site of the present Parasol's Bar. The station's entire format consisted of Irish movies and cooking shows. Viewers lost interest, however, with the advent of color television when management insisted on broadcasting only in green.

• Fats Domino founded Antoine's restaurant. Fats, whose real name is Antoine, even created a dessert dish that was on the restaurant's original menu — a huge berry dumpling known as the blueberry hill.

• "Bananas" Foster was the name of a notorious New Orleans gangster of the 1920s. "Bananas," whose trademark was a bright yellow suit, was so mean that he once doused an ice cream wagon with rum and set it on fire. His career came to an end when he ran afoul of a rival French Quarter gang headed by the notorious "Oysters" Rockefeller.

• In New Orleans, if a legend and a banana tree are planted side by side at the same time, the legend will spread faster than the banana tree.

IN MEMORY

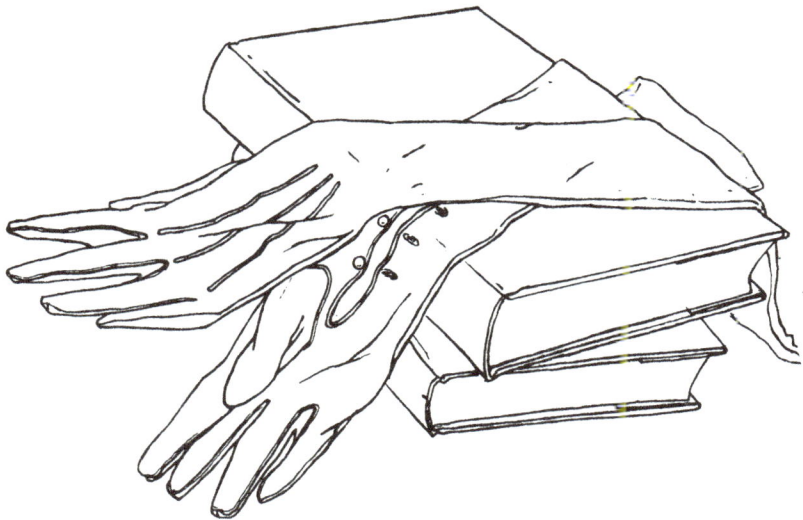

Thelma

What came to mind first was the mints. That was what I left with the first time I visited Thelma Toole. She was a grand lady who deemed it a quite polite gesture to give her guests a gift. As I left she handed me a D.H. Holmes bag; the bag contained a box of chocolate-covered mints — the box had remains of a price tag, from Schwegmann's.

That was the sort of life that Thelma Toole lived, pure New Orleanian, a cross between a D.H. Holmes style and a Schwegmann's pocketbook. She lived in a simple shotgun home on Elysian Fields near Rampart but her character was more St. Charles near Napoleon.

She was a gifted woman, well-schooled in music and literature. To entertain company she might perform briefly on her piano or sing a few lines from some long-remembered poem. In another century, Thelma Toole would have made a grand plantation lady, charming the local planters and their wives at a time when genteel conversation made for an evening's entertainment. Such a persona was lodged in the spirit of a woman who in the 1980s still considered it inappropriate to appear in public without white gloves and a hat.

But the lady was also a fighter, and it is for that she will be best remembered. One of the most inspiring footnotes to contemporary American literature has to be the story of Thelma Toole's tenacity in getting *A Confederacy of Dunces* — the manuscript by her deceased son, John Kennedy Toole — published, distributed and promoted. It was the battle of her adult life, and she won.

As the book became famous, so did Thelma, in her self-appointed capacity as her son's publicist. She was proof that a diamond in the rough is a diamond nonetheless, as she rather suddenly assumed the role of celebrity. Reporters waited for interviews. NBC flew her to New York for an appearance on the Tomorrow Show. Johnny Carson called to ask about movie rights for *Confederacy*. The block on Elysian Fields near Rampart, along which elderly people push shopping carts from the nearby Schwegmann's, had suddenly become a literary curiosity.

Thelma put on her hat and gloves more frequently as she met the demand for personal appearances, telling crowds at libraries and social clubs about her son and the saga of getting his book published. published. Some saw her as a calculating woman merely cashing in on another's work. But those who spent some time with her knew better. There were financial rewards from the book's sale, but to an old lady who needed a walker for mobility it was too late for money to make much difference. Her objective was to let the world know about her son — the author.

There were other memories that came to mind last week at the news of Thelma's death at 82. One was of her showing me a picture of the pretty young grammar school teacher that she once was. The teacher would become so enamored with her infant son's education that she would write a series of poems for him to read. There was both sadness and pride in her voice as the elderly Thelma re-read those poems written to interest her favorite pupil in the splendor of words.

Another memory was of a dusty, wingbacked chair in the corner of the front room in her home. In response to one of my questions she pointed me towards the chair. Mixed in the clutter on the seat was a folder which I opened. The citation within had recently been awarded posthumously to John Kennedy Toole and read — Pulitzer Prize for Literature.

Thelma Toole's little house on Elysian Fields would have something on the wall not found in even the grandest of homes.

Angelo

Angelo Brocato Jr. never had to spend too much time worrying about career planning. He was born adjacent to Poppa Angelo's Italian ice cream business 68 years ago, began sweeping the floors there as a child, started serving tables at 12 and eventually took over the business.

"What do you do, when you're not working?" I once asked Brocato. "I feel like I'm lost," he answered.

"Do you plan to retire soon?"

"No," Brocato replied, "as long as I'm living, I don't think I'll retire."

True to his word, Brocato worked all his life. He died early on the morning of Oct. 7, 1982, ironically on the eve of the Columbus Day weekend, a weekend of celebration for the **American-Italian** community when the city's Sicilian heritage was in its glory and passersby could have munched on fig cookies and spumoni from the Brocato's food booth at the Piazza d'Italia.

Angelo Brocato Jr. was a witness to that heritage. He was raised in the Quarter, back in the days when Sicilians turned the cluster of narrow streets and shotgun houses into their very own neighborhood. Little Angelo watched his father, whom he described as "a hard-working man," bake cookies and make ice cream during the daylight, then serve customers at night.

Angelo Sr. was one of the Sicilian success stories. Like many turn-of-the-century Italians, he came to Louisiana to work in the sugar cane fields. But since he had had experience in the ice cream business back in his native Palermo, he moved to New Orleans to open his own shop, right in the heart of the Italian sector, on Ursulines Street.

Angelo Jr. recalled some of his father's stories about early life in the **New Orleans Italian** community. There were the sunny days, for instance, when Italian men would compete with each other by trying to climb greased poles. There were tales of life in Sicily where Angelo Sr. took his family for 18 months when little Angelo was eight.

Angelo Jr. had his memories too, such as evenings when he and his brothers would provided curb service for the cars parked along Ursulines Street. "Most people don't remember that," Brocato remembered, "but we used to have trays and everything that we would carry to people in their cars, just like what they used to have at the old Morning Call."

Then there were the customers. Brocato remembered that movie stars came in, although he was too young to know who they were. He did remember the prize fighters though. The Quarter once bred boxers at the gym at St. Mary's Italian church where tough Italian boys were taught to fight by the rules. It was natural that a Quarter kid would be impressed when brawlers like World Middleweight Champion Tony Canizzanaro walked through the doors.

In the early days, those doors opened early each morning to provide what became half of a favored but forgotten New Orleans Sicilian breakfast. Neighbors would begin their day by going to Central Grocery on Decatur for a loaf of warm Italian bread, then head to Brocato's and plop down a nickel for a glass of lemon ice where they sat at the shop's tiny tables and dipped pieces of bread into the ice. "You wouldn't believe how good that was," Brocato mentioned. "I remember Diamond Jim Moran used to send his sons in each morning with a pitcher to fill with lemon ice."

Through the years lemon ice has been the staple of the business. In another time, it was the cannoli — a tube-shaped pastry stuffed with sweetened ricotta cheese. Then there are the ice creams — cassata, spumoni and terroncino—all made on the premises, many with flavorings imported from Sicily. There were more seasonal variations back then. Cannolis were served from October through Easter. Then Easter until the following October the kitchens would churn out the rich ice creams. "Some places make five gallons of ice cream and stretch it into ten," Brocato lectured, "we don't do that, we don't have any overrun. Ours is a more solid ice cream. We may have to charge a little more, but we give quality."

Brocato recalled that tastes changed with time. His father once made a strawberry ice, but it was not popular in the Italian neighborhood. Recently, the shop reintroduced the dish and it has become one of the top sellers. He explained that the now ethnically-mixed generation of customers prefers the likes of strawberry ice and chocolate and vanilla ice creams, while terrancino—a traditional Sicilian ice cream with great almond and cinnamon flavor, is not as popular as it once was.

More than tastes have changed through the years — the Brocato brothers went different ways. James started his own shop near St. Claude, and Angelo maintained his father's business. The original store Quarter was eventually closed in favor of a place on North Carrollton Ave. operated by Arthur, the youngest of Angelo Jr.'s sons. At its new location, the business has been such a success that it recently had to expand.

But other things have remained the same. The neon sign still hangs outside the shop. There is still a white tile floor, and lightbulbs still outline the blue ceiling overhang. Most of all, customers are still keeping the doors swinging. The one noticeable difference is that

Angelo Brocato Jr. isn't behind the counter anymore.

Brocato got to see three generations of prosperity for the business his father stated. Of him it can be said that he continued the tradition. Given the everyday demise of things worth saving, that in itself was a noble accomplishment.

Big Maybelle

They buried Big Maybelle last week and her funeral was quite a scene. Traffic along Toledano Street was slowed to the pace of a jazz band — "The Original Sixth Ward Dirty Dozen." The group had the honor of leading Maybelle's jazz send-off.

A hundred or so people marched, skipped and danced alongside the hearse. Folks who live along the street were drawn from their bungalows by the sound of the approaching band. A class of school-girls, in parochial grey skirts and checkered coats, watched from the neutral ground. They were having a field trip into folk culture.

I don't know much about Big Maybelle except for information volunteered by a girl who was second-lining. The girl, like most good second- liners, was waving an umbrella, and she managed to lower it to half-mast long enough to explain that the deceased was no ordinary Big Maybelle. No, she was "The Original Big Maybelle," and long, long ago she performed at the city's now defunct incubator for black blues, The Dew Drop Inn. That said, the girl raised her umbrella and continued her strutting.

Meanwhile, I was left with images of a person I had never met nor seen: Steamy nights on the stage at the Dew Drop. There's Big Maybelle wailing, her songs slowed by the humidity. Dudes in zoot suits are looking for sparks and Maybelle's providing the electricity.

There were plenty memories and as Maybelle aged, the memories got stronger. Perhaps from time to time Maybelle and the former dudes and their gals would happen to meet. They would laugh and remember about the times of their lives most worth remembering. They would run through the list of characters, chuckle at the night when. . . and ask, what ever happened to. . . ? After a while, the latter question was asked less often as the obituary page became more a part of the answer. But there was no time for death when there was so much living to remember.

It may have been that some of Maybelle's now-elderly fans were walking along with the procession or waiting at the church. They were seeing her go out as they had first seen her, amidst dancing people and a blaze of music.

Those fans can take heart that at least Maybelle had the good fortune to die in New Orleans — a place where custom allowed her death to be mourned yet celebrated as a tribute to what her life had brought. There was nothing somber about Maybelle's jazz funeral, but then there probably wasn't much somber about Maybelle, either.

For the record, it can be reported that Maybelle was buried on a beautiful Monday morning. The procession moved down Toledano, across Claiborne, then turned along a segment of Willow Street that runs through the Magnolia project. Even the project looked good that morning as the jazz ricocheted from the faded orange bricks. Within the project the marchers increased, as did the tempo. The celebrants were chanting and dancing towards the cemetery. Maybelle's journey was almost complete, but oh didn't she ramble.

There will still be quiet evenings when the old-timers from the Dew Drop will happen to meet. They'll still recall the list of characters. They'll still chuckle at the nights when. . . They'll still laugh. They'll still remember.

Whatever happened to Big Maybelle?

She'll be marchin' in with the saints now.

James Booker

Allan Toussaint was on the stage of the Maple Leaf Bar playing some rollicking boogie-woogie. The person next to me, a writer, held up one finger and whispered, in reference to Toussaint, "There's only one genius left now." The other genius was James Booker, whose death was the reason for that evening's memorial at the Leaf. It was a Monday evening, the time of the week when Booker would ordinarily be behind the piano for his weekly gig at the bar. Instead, performers were donating their time both to honor the man and to help raise money for a suitable tombstone.

Earlier in the evening there had been a spot of poetry and then a couple of renditions of "Sunny Side of the Street," one of Booker's more conventional standards. Later an improvised band led by Deacon John assembled on the stage for a few oldies and some heavy rock. Those who remembered Deacon John from their high school days might not have expected the electric wailing from his guitar. But where life goes on, things change, even amidst memories such as when

Mr. Google Eyes, one of the local rhythm and blues relics, sang out the lyrics to, "It's Something You've Got." The crowd, by this time beer-crazy, joined in the chorus, "My, my. Oh, oh. I love you so."

It went on into the wee hours, when saxophonists Red Tyler and Earl King offered their tributes. Like soldiers who honor a fallen comrade with gun salutes, musicians were honoring one of their own with their tools, their music.

Throughout the evening, passersby along Oak Street stopped to stare through the streetside windows which opened to the back of the tiny stage. It reminded me of the one time I saw Booker perform. Walking from the restaurant next door, I was attracted by the melody coming from the Leaf. Staring in through those windows, I could see Booker behind his piano playing, and singing a sad, soulful version of "Oh, Holy Night" before a nearly empty house. His audience was seldom large, and his music that evening was the moving sound of a lonely person — lonely but exploding with emotion.

There was a wealth of live talent for the memorial but the main attraction came from a videotape shown on a television set that was rolled on stage. The tape was of a concert Booker had staged only weeks earlier, before the cameras of Cox Cable, on that very stage at the Maple Leaf. The piano, minus its player, provided the background for the performance on the screen.

One hundred or so people in a bar could not be expected to sit patiently and stare at a screen for a half-hour, but many did, watching Booker give a fine performance. His feelings were high as he continued to grin at the cameras, providing what will now be an unforgettable glimpse of himself. His hands were full of razzle-dazzle as he slid from one song to another. After each set, those watching the television applauded as though this were an ordinary Monday evening at the Leaf. People were dancing, including his two aunts, one of whom kept shaking a finger at the screen as though to encourage her nephew to keep up the rhythm. The evening was a fitting gesture which made it possible to say that the last time James Booker was seen playing at the Maple Leaf the house was full and his music was splendid.

Chase's New Orleans

John Chase was a type of journalist rarely seen anymore, a person with a passionate and scholarly interest in the history of his city. He was a great storyteller, with the added ability to tell stories unlike anyone else, through his own illustrations of the city's life. Several generations of New Orleanians formed their images of the city's past by the perspective from Chase's pen.

If Chase had done nothing else in life than just draw cartoons, that alone would have qualified him as a major figure in the city's journalistic history. His newspaper cartoons, with the *New Orleans States* and then the *States-Item*, were the most insightful, witty and stylish in town. Chase's "Little Man" character, complete with an oversized hat and a brush-like moustache, became a symbol for the New Orleanian, sometimes frustrated and overwhelmed by events but always able to rejoice as needed. After a career as a newspaper cartoonist Chase retired, during which time he was frequently called upon to provide the artwork for various public events and charitable causes. The "Little Man," who by then deserved a leisurely retirement himself, was put to work as a civic do-gooder.

There was no mystery, however, in the "Little Man's" civic pride, considering, after all, who his pen-mates were. He shared the artist's pad with the likes of Bienville, Lafitte, Andy Jackson and all the other characters from the city's past who were born again through Chase. The cartoonist's images were sometimes too big for a simple newspaper space, so it was only right that it was Chase who was called upon to do the splendid historical mural in the lobby of the main library. Libraries open and close and their hours are shortened, but at least Chase opened the way for a peek at the past.

As a cartoonist, Chase not only dealt with history; he made it himself, becoming the first-ever television editorial cartoonist. For several years his illustrations punctuated the end of the newscasts on WDSU, Channel 6. TV technology even allowed the characters to occasionally do something they had never done before — to move. When hurricanes were coming, or the parade crowds were too large, the Little Man finally had the legs to move out of the way.

Chase will be remembered not just for pictures, but for words as well. He was a historian, not just a storyteller (an important distinction in a city where many so-called "historians" just recite tired and untested yarns), who made an important contribution to the literature of the city. His book, *Frenchmen, Desire, Good Children, and Other Streets of New Orleans*, besides having one of the most clever titles to ever hit local bookshelves, is the classic study of the city's street names. It is a lively book overflowing with stories about developers, landowners, plantation masters, politicians and all those who shared the character and place-names of the city's neighborhoods. In a sense it is a perfect historical book, well-researched, dealing with an otherwise overlooked topic and written and illustrated in such a way as to make it appealing to a large audience. Whenever, in the future, local history will be studied, Chase will be one of the sources.

Fortune had it that in his last years Chase was able to see his book presented in a way that was totally appropriate to him. For the 1985 Mardi Gras, the Krewe of Proteus adopted *Frenchmen, Desire, Good Children* as its theme. As the story goes, Chase had been ailing during the planning of the parade, but as it approached he suddenly found new spirit, even bringing in family members from out of town to see the spectacle. At an autograph party for the krewe, Chase even found the stamina to sign nearly 500 copies of the book.

At the time of his death, Chase was working on a book about the arrival, in 1699, of the first Frenchmen to the mouth of the Mississippi. The fact that that date, March 3, will also be the date of next year's Mardi Gras added to his enthusiasm. It was the sort of subtle observation that only someone with Chase's compassion for New Orleans would notice. Sadly, there will now be fewer people noticing such things, and fewer stories being told.

About the Author

Errol Laborde describes himself as a committed urban dweller whose beat to date has been his native city of New Orleans. He is the publisher and editor of *Louisiana Life* magazine and a columnist for *City Business*. His "Streetcar" column, which began running weekly in *Gambit* in 1982, is now found monthly in *New Orleans Magazine*, where he also serves as associate publisher and editor. Producer and panelist for the television program *Informed Sources*, Laborde has taught political science at local universities and founded several community projects, including the Tennessee Williams/New Orleans Literary Festival. He also gives talks on state and local politics, as well as on the history of Mardi Gras.

TYPOGRAPHER'S NOTE

The text is set in 10-point Palatino, first cut in 1950 by Hermann Zapf, one of this century's most accomplished type designers. While its large x-height lends a modern legibility, its design — particularly evident in the italics — harkens back to the imitation of handwriting that was the hallmark of the very earliest typefaces. The combination of readability and elegance has made Palatino one of the most popular text typefaces. The type was set by "Lars," an antique phototypesetting machine which itself has had quite a career in New Orleans alternative journalism. The large chapter headings were set by hand in Wave, a typeface I find suggestive of the cast-iron balconies for which the French Quarter is justly celebrated. — *T.F.*

www.ingramcontent.com/pod-product-compliance
Lightning Source LLC
LaVergne TN
LVHW011236080426
835509LV00005B/530